Nāgārjuna's Verses
on the Great Vehicle
and
the Heart of Dependent Origination

Nāgārjuna's Verses
on the Great Vehicle
and
the Heart of Dependent Origination

by

R.C. Jamieson

D.K. Printworld (P) Ltd.
New Delhi - 110 015

Cataloging in Publication Data — DK

Jamieson, R.C. (R. Craig)

Nāgārjuna's verses on the great vehicle and the heart of dependent origination.
Includes bibliographical references and index.

1. Nāgārjuna, 2nd cent. Mahāyānaviṁśaka. 2. Nāgārjuna, 2nd cent. Pratītyasamutpādahṛdayakārikā. 3. Mādhyamika (Buddhism). 4. Pratītyasamutpāda. 5. Mahayana Buddhism — Doctrines. I. Nāgārjuna, 2nd cent. Mahāyānaviṁśaka. English & Tibetan. II. Nāgārjuna, 2nd cent. Pratīyasamutpādahṛdayakīrikā. English & Tibetan.

Originally published (*in 2000 by* Peter Lang Publishing, Inc., NewYork) ***as:*** A study of Nāgārjuna's Twenty verses on the Great Vehicle (Mahāyānaviṁśikā) and his verses on the heart of dependent origination (Pratītyasamutapādahṛdayakārikā) with the interpretation of the heart of dependent origination (Pratītyasamutpādahṛdayavyākhyāna), (Toronto studies in religion; vol. 15).

ISBN81-246-0175-5
First Indian edition 2001

This edition is published by arrangement with Peter Lang Publishing, Inc., New York. It is for sale in India, Nepal and Bhutan only.

Published and printed in India by:
D.K. Printworld (P) Ltd.
Regd. office: *'Sri Kunj'*, F-52, Bali Nagar
New Delhi - 110015
Phone: (011) 545-3975, 546-6019; *Fax*: (011) 546-5926
E-Mail: dkprint@4mis.com

TO SHIRLEY,

whose vitality brought me insights
I might never have seen.

Acknowledgements

By way of acknowledgements there are quite a few people who deserve thanks in one way or another. Professor Emeritus David Snellgrove was influential in the early stages of this and related work. Dr Friedhelm Hardy was my first serious teacher of Sanskrit. Professor Emeritus J.W. de Jong gave his detailed comments and encouragement in the final stages of the work. Diana and Dick St. Ruth drew my attention to the need for accessible translations of these particular texts. Marianne Winder has proofread and commented upon the Tibetan throughout the book. Thupten Jinpa also proofread the book and gave valuable comment on the Tibetan especially. Nick Smith and Thirza Hope have proofread the non-Tibetan parts of the book. Thanks are also due to Michel Garel and the staff of the Division orientale of the Département des Manuscrits in the Bibliothèque Nationale, Paris, and to Graham Shaw and the staff of Oriental Collections in the British Library, London. Rosemary Rodd did a wonderful job transferring the whole book from one computer system to another in order to provide fonts of the quality required by the publisher. Much of this took place while I was away from Cambridge, in India, or when I was ill, so much more of this very fiddly task fell on her than should have done. Particular thanks to Don Weibe the editor of the series Toronto Studies In Religion, for his supportive enthusiasm for this book at all stages. Thanks also to Jacqueline Pavlovic and everyone else at Lang for their support in the publication process. And most importantly Shirley Jamieson has helped in countless ways.

Preface

The purpose of the translation provided in part one is to present Buddhist texts in an accessible form unencumbered by critical apparatus. Part two provides text-critical material as well as other comment for readers interested in more than the unembellished translation in isolation. Part three provides further text-critical material and other comment in the light of the Dunhuang manuscripts which relate to the Pratītyasamutpādahṛdaya.

Footnotes, comment, references, bibliographic detail and so on can often obscure a text. The academic reader may become entranced by the scholarship displayed at the expense of content, while non-academic readers may simply decide that the work — worthy as it might be for advancing knowledge about the literature — is irrelevant and unapproachable from their point of view. The most eminent sinologist in fiction, Professor Peter Klein in Elias Canetti's *Auto da Fé*, presumably had a nominal readership for his exceedingly erudite work and would have been worried had it been otherwise. Of course he also receives his just deserts. His was not an ideal for which everyone would wish to strive. Be that as it may, perhaps a middle way can be found between a wooden and impenetrable but pedantically sound literalness in the approach to a text and, at the other extreme, a readable *translation* only very loosely based on an original source. Hopefully it will be worthwhile for those willing to make use of it. If it is not in accordance with your own notions bear in mind that it is simply what is judged to be helpful for those who have the curiosity to learn more about Buddhism's Nāgārjuna.

Contents

Part 1

English translation

Introduction to the Mahāyānaviṃśikā

The Mahāyānaviṃśikā is attributed to Nāgārjuna in its Chinese and Tibetan versions, as well as elsewhere in Tibetan tradition. Christian Lindtner in his discussion of the authenticity of this attribution cites the Caryāmelāyanapradīpa, the Tattvasārasaṃgraha and Atīśa's Bodhimārgadīpapañjikā as ascribing the work to him, and classes the text's attribution to Nāgārjuna as "*perhaps* authentic".[1] This is a safe course; there is nothing to suggest attribution to another later Nāgārjuna, but equally there is nothing which altogether eliminates such a possibility. Many will feel the "perhaps" is rather a strong one, as the text is often clumsy, it was not mentioned by Candrakīrti, and could so easily have been compiled at a late date and then ascribed to Nāgārjuna.

The Mahāyānaviṃśikā translated here is largely that of the Tibetan tradition, a version translated into Tibetan by the Kashmiri paṇḍit Ānanda and the Tibetan translator Grags 'byor shes rab.

Differences between versions of the Mahāyānaviṃśikā available to us are not limited to an occasional variant reading here and there. The number of verses, the order of the verses, and the presence of particular verses differ from version to version. The other Tibetan translation by the Indian paṇḍit Candrakumāra and the Tibetan translator Sha' kya 'od has twenty-three verses. There is a Chinese translation by Shih hu (Dānapāla) which has twenty-four verses. There is also a text in Sanskrit — the language of the original — which at first sight has twenty-eight verses.

Our translation is not a wholesale reconstruction of an original text gleaned from the various versions, but some have seen it as to some extent an attempt to put into readable English the content of Nāgārjuna's text as it might have been at a stage much earlier than any of the surviving manuscripts. Such a claim may not bear serious consideration and is certainly not the sort of thing that can be proven. What is offered here is a simple translation based on the rather mechanical Tibetan translation made by Ānanda and Grags 'byor shes rab of their Sanskrit original, leavened with a certain amount of the very readable Tibetan translation made by

1 Lindtner, Christian; Nagarjuniana : studies in the writings and philosophy of Nāgārjuna, Copenhagen, 1982, p. 12.

Candrakumāra and Sha' kya 'od of their Sanskrit original, always in the light of the one particular Sanskrit manuscript which has come down to us. The thinking behind what elements are favoured in particular instances should be clear enough in the footnotes to the edited Tibetan and in the text-critical material which follows it. The difference in approach between the two Tibetan translations is both interesting and significant. That significance is discussed after the presentation of the two Tibetan versions. Our translation consists of twenty verses, which matches rather neatly the title Mahāyānaviṃśikā, literally "The Great Vehicle in Twenty Parts", suggesting "Twenty Verses on the Great Vehicle".

The style of the verses is such that a certain attentiveness is required when reading them. The verses were composed in a way which combats the tendency to see what is expected, what is run of the mill, rather than what is actually there. The turns of phrase, the particular constructions, reflect an attempt to reward attentive reading; the ideas are mainstream Buddhism yet the style is both fresh and lively as well as authoritative. However, the style of the original is one of the things inevitably diluted — if not lost — in translation.

Our translation of the text — setting it apart from some other versions — opens with the expected verse of invocation, and then continues by saying that both, Buddhas and sentient beings, all have the same characteristics, characteristics which are much like space, not arising and not becoming extinct. In the sphere of omniscient knowledge even mental activities are void; they have arisen in interdependence upon each other, much like the two banks of a river. All existence is essentially considered to resemble a reflected image — pure, tranquil in its self-nature, non-dual, and resembling its true nature. Ordinary people think there is a self in what is without self, and that enjoyment, suffering, impartiality and defilements are all real. They think that in worldly existence there are six destinies, in heaven there is ultimate enjoyment, in hell there is great suffering, and in an object there is inconceivable truth. However, unpleasantness, suffering, aging, and disease are impermanent, and the result of actions is both enjoyment and suffering. Someone deluded in worldly existence is much like a painter frightening himself with a terrifying image of a goblin, a picture which he himself has created. Sentient beings sink into the mud of false imagining, from which it is so difficult for them to extricate themselves, much as someone foolish might fall into mud he himself has made. Seeing the non-existent as existing, a feeling of suffering is experienced, and their mistaken anxieties trouble them with the poison of apprehension. Buddhas, with their minds steeped in compassion, seeing these defenceless sentient beings and acting for their benefit, urge them towards perfect enlightenment. Once their merit is accumulated, after attaining supreme knowledge, and disentangled from the net of imagining, they may become Buddhas, friends of the world. Because of seeing the true meaning, people accordingly have knowledge, and then the world is seen as void, without beginning, middle or end. They do not themselves see either worldly existence or nirvāṇa, which is unspoiled, unchanging, originally tranquil and resplendent. Someone awakened from the sleep of delusion no longer sees worldly existence, much as someone awakened no longer sees an object experienced in a dream. Those perceiving permanence, self and enjoyment, among things which are without self-nature, drift about in this ocean of existence, surrounded by the darkness of delusion and attachment. Just as they imagine the world, people themselves have not arisen. Beyond its imagined arising this has no meaning. This is all just thought, produced like a conjuring act; from it there is good and bad action, and from that there is good and bad birth. If this wheel of thought disappears, then the essence of all things disappears. There is no self in the true nature of things; that is the purity of the true nature of things. Who, without embarking on the Great Vehicle, could cross over to the other shore of the vast ocean of worldly existence full to overflowing with imagining?

Twenty Verses on the Great Vehicle

The Sanskrit

Mahāyānaviṃśikā

The Tibetan

theg pa chen po ni nyi shu pa

Homage to the three jewels.

Homage to the inconceivably powerful Buddha, his understanding free from ties;
By whose uttered teachings the unutterable is taught out of kindness.

Buddhas and sentient beings have the same characteristics, which are much like space;
Essentially they do not arise, and in truth they do not become extinct.

In the sphere of omniscient knowledge even mental activities are void,
Much like the two banks of a river, they have arisen, essentially born of interdependence.

All existence is essentially considered to resemble a reflected image,
Pure, tranquil in its self-nature, non-dual, and resembling its true nature.

Ordinary people think there is a self in what is without self,
And that enjoyment, suffering, impartiality and defilements, all of these are real.

In worldly existence there are six destinies, and in heaven there is ultimate enjoyment,
In hell there is great suffering, and in an object there is inconceivable truth.

However, unpleasantness, suffering, aging, and disease are
impermanent,
And the result of actions is both enjoyment and suffering.

Someone deluded in worldly existence is much like a painter
Frightening himself with a terrifying image of a goblin he himself
has created.

Sentient beings sink into the mud of false imagining, from which it
is difficult to extricate themselves,
Much as someone foolish might fall into mud he himself has made.

Seeing the non-existent as existing, a feeling of suffering is
experienced;
Their mistaken anxieties trouble them with the poison of
apprehension.

Buddhas, with their minds steeped in compassion, seeing these
defenceless sentient beings,
And acting for their benefit, urge them towards perfect
enlightenment.

Their merit accumulated, after attaining supreme knowledge,
Disentangled from the net of imagining, may they become Buddhas,
friends of the world.

Because of seeing the true meaning, people accordingly have
knowledge,
Then the world is seen as void, without beginning, middle or end.

They do not themselves see either worldly existence or nirvāṇa,
Which is unspoiled, unchanging, originally tranquil and resplendent.

Someone awakened from the sleep of delusion no longer sees worldly existence,
Much as someone awakened no longer sees an object experienced in a dream.

Those perceiving permanence, self and enjoyment, among things which are without self-nature,
Drift about in this ocean of existence, surrounded by the darkness of delusion and attachment.

Just as they imagine the world, people themselves have not arisen,
Beyond its imagined arising this has no meaning.

This is all just thought, produced like a conjuring act;
From it there is good and bad action, and from that there is good and bad birth.

If this wheel of thought disappears, then the essence of all things disappears,
There is no self in the true nature of things; that is the purity of the true nature of things.

Who, without embarking on the Great Vehicle, could cross over to the other shore
Of the vast ocean of worldly existence full to overflowing with imagining?

* * * * *

Twenty Verses on the Great Vehicle by the noble learned teacher Nāgārjuna, translated by the Kashmiri paṇḍit Ānanda and the translator monk Grags 'byor shes rab.

Introduction to the Pratītyasamutpādahṛdayakārikā and its Pratītyasamutpādahṛdayavyākhyāna

"The Verses on the Heart of Dependent Origination" (Pratītyasamutpādahṛdayakārikā) and "An Interpretation of the Heart of Dependent Origination" (Pratītyasamutpādahṛdayavyākhyāna) are both attributed to Nāgārjuna in Chinese and Tibetan versions.

The inclusion here of a translated commentary with the verses may come as a surprise, and certainly the change of style when turning from verses to prose commentary is a considerable jolt. Much of the reason so little commentarial literature is translated is because the style can seem unapproachable, conforming to an Indian tradition quite different to any popular English prose. At times a commentary can be so succinct as to resemble writing in note form. It can make points hinging on the grammar of the text which can be only very artificially reflected in translation. It can explain points which are rather obvious in one place while elsewhere it will take for granted knowledge common to all of its expected readers. In translation the needs of the reader can be quite different, so often commentaries are paraphrased, skipping obvious statements and pedantic concerns while expanding points which may be unclear to an audience unfamiliar with elementary Buddhist literature.

Including the commentary in a form which reflects the Indian style may jar at first, but it provides an authentic example of one commentary for those who do not read the languages in which these texts are preserved. The pedantic nature of such writing means that many points are clarified without overmuch concern about how obvious they may or may not be. For example our verses take for granted that the standard twelve specific component parts of dependent origination are well known, indeed it cites numbers only, whereas my translation makes the concession of including the terms themselves. An authentic translation looks extremely daunting even to those to whom the twelve are well known in the standard order: ignorance, mental activities, consciousness, name and form, the six bases of sense perception, touch, feeling, craving, grasping, existence, birth, and aging and death.

> "The first, eighth and ninth come under defilement, the second and tenth come under action,
> While the remaining seven come under suffering — hence twelve phenomena can be treated as three.
> Out of this threefold twofold originates; out of this twofold sevenfold originates;
> And out of this sevenfold threefold originates; that is the wheel of existence turning again and again."

Another Indian tradition, that of skilful memorizing, cannot now automatically be taken for granted, but commentary writers could not have been expected to foresee such a development. However, by their comprehensive annotation of so many points even the modern reader with a lazy memory is aided, and in fact our commentary helpfully attaches the expected words to each of the numbers.

The explanation provided varies considerably. While our commentary will not say that each reference in these texts to 'the Sage', 'the Instructor', 'the Tathāgata', and so on refers to Śākyamuni Buddha, as that point is too obvious to the commentator and his expected readers, it will say quite elementary things, such as that the five components of personal existence are form, feeling, perception, mental activities and consciousness. In looking at the commentary it can be seen that such emphasis does serve to keep the elements of the verse being explained in mind so that — continuing with this example — five causes can be referred to without mentioning components of personal existence in the same phrase, but the reader knows that in this instance, explaining this verse, the five causes are the five components of personal existence.

Commentators try to anticipate possible areas of doubt or hazy recollection, but not lack of familiarity with matters Indian or Buddhist. For example a division of existence into desire, form and formlessness would automatically suggest the sphere of sense desire which includes all states of existence, including sentient beings and certain gods, up to and including the paranirmitavaśavartin gods, the sphere of form which is the sphere where the various rūpāvacara gods are found, and the sphere of formlessness which is the sphere where the various ārūpyāvacara gods are found. When a tripod is mentioned, photography cannot be in mind; instead the three-staved tripod on which a religious mendicant places his water pot serves as the illustration. And that there should be anyone who does not know the taste of tamarind sauce would most certainly surprise an Indian commentator.

Our translation of the text opens with the statement of intent, that the twelve specific component parts which the Sage called dependent origination can be fully treated as three: defilement, action and suffering. Ignorance (the first in the cycle), craving (the eighth) and grasping (the ninth) come under defilement. Mental activities (the second) and existence (the tenth) come under action. The remaining seven — consciousness, name and form, the six bases of sense perception, touch, feeling, birth, and aging and death — come under suffering. Hence twelve phenomena can be treated as three. Out of this threefold defilement twofold action originates. Out of this twofold action sevenfold suffering originates. Out of this sevenfold suffering threefold defilement originates. That is the wheel of existence turning again and again. The whole world is just cause and effect, and a sentient being is no different. Phenomena which are void simply originate out of phenomena which are void. In recitation, in a lamp, in a mirror, in a seal, in a rock-crystal lens, in a seed, in a tamarind, in a shout, and even in the transmigration of the components of personal existence, the learned understand that there is no transference taking place. But the ignorant, who imagine even the most subtle thing can come to an end, do not see the significance of origination from attendant causes. There is nothing to be taken away and nothing at all to be added here; the truth should be seen as truth and anyone who sees the truth is released.

Verses on the Heart of Dependent Origination

The Sanskrit

Pratītyasamutpādahṛdayakārikā

The Tibetan

rten cing 'brel par 'byung ba'i
snying po'i tshig le'ur byas pa

Homage to the ever youthful Mañjuśrī.

The twelve specific component parts, which the Sage called dependent origination,
Can be fully treated as three: defilement, action and suffering.

The first (ignorance), eighth (craving) and ninth (grasping) come under defilement; the second (mental activities) and tenth (existence) come under action,
While the remaining seven (consciousness, name and form, the six bases of sense perception, touch, feeling, birth, and aging and death) come under suffering — hence twelve phenomena can be treated as three.

Out of this threefold defilement twofold action originates; out of this twofold action sevenfold suffering originates;
And out of this sevenfold suffering threefold defilement originates; that is the wheel of existence turning again and again.

The whole world is just cause and effect, and a sentient being is no different.
Phenomena which are void simply originate out of phenomena which are void.

In recitation, in a lamp, in a mirror, in a seal, in a rock-crystal lens, in a seed, in a tamarind, in a shout,
And even in the transmigration of the components of personal existence, the learned understand that there is no transference taking place.

But the ignorant, who imagine even the most subtle thing can come to an end,
Do not see the significance of origination from attendant causes.

There is nothing to be taken away and nothing at all to be added
here;
The truth should be seen as truth and anyone who sees the truth is
released.

* * * * *

Verses on the Heart of Dependent Origination by the noble learned teacher Nāgārjuna.

An Interpretation of the Heart of Dependent Origination

The Sanskrit

Pratītyasamutpādahṛdayavyākhyāna

The Tibetan

rten cing 'brel par 'byung ba'i
snying po'i rnam par bshad pa

Homage to the ever youthful Mañjuśrī.

Here an attentive monk, a listening, understanding, retentive, aware, astute, an authoritative pupil, approached the learned teacher beginning his explanation of the Tathāgata's doctrine, and asked him: "Blessed One, with regard to '*The twelve specific component parts, which the Sage called dependent origination*', I wish to hear how they can be considered in an abridged form."

Understanding his desire to know the essence of these teachings, the learned teacher said that they '*Can be fully treated as three: defilement, action and suffering*'.

Clarifying that, he gave the following outline: "The full number of them is twelve. The component parts, in that they are specific ones, are the specific component parts which can be explained as being component parts much like the component parts of a cart. A 'sage' is the result of sagacity in body and speech. The phrase 'the Sage called...' refers to the categories of his narration and his elucidation. This dependent origination is not born of causes such as inherent nature, certainty, man, reliance on others, an omnipotent being, time, intrinsic nature, capriciousness, chance, misery and so on. Those twelve specific component parts fully treated as three — defilement, action and suffering — are mutually dependent, a sort of tripod. They are 'fully treated' in that the complete significance is conveyed."

He asked, "What are the defilements? What are actions? What is suffering? How are the specific dependent things abridged?"

He replied, " '*The first, eighth and ninth come under defilement*'. The first of the specific twelve is ignorance. The eighth is craving. The ninth is grasping. These three should be known as defilements.

What are actions? '*...the second and tenth come under action*'. The second is mental activities. The tenth is existence. These two phenomena should be known as abridged under action.

'*While the remaining seven come under suffering*'. Those which are the seven specific ones remaining after those abridged under defilement and action, should be known as abridged under suffering. They are: consciousness, name and form, the six bases of sense perception, touch, feeling, birth, and aging and death. The words of the verse can be regarded as tying up loose ends. The sufferings of those deprived of the pleasant, meeting with the unpleasant, and not getting what is wanted are combined.

'... — *hence twelve phenomena can be treated as three*'. Therefore these twelve phenomena should be known as actions, defilements and sufferings.

But the words suggest the complete meaning. There is nothing at all varying from the teachings described in the Sūtras.

He asked, "That ascertained, explain these defilements, actions and sufferings, what has arisen and from where?"

He replied, " '*Out of this threefold twofold originates*'. Out of this threefold defilement twofold action originates. '*...out of this twofold sevenfold originates*', which is suffering, as described above. '*And out of this sevenfold threefold originates*', which is defilements, and out of that threefold defilement twofold action originates. '*...that is the wheel of existence turning again and again*'. That threefold existence is called desire, form and formlessness. Among those this world of ordinary people wanders about, an unceasing wheel. The words of the verse mean transience is suggested. Though in various existences it may not be understood that the wheel turns steadily, he teaches that it is transient.

He asked, "Then what is the lord of all bodies, which is called a sentient being? How does it operate?"

He replied, " '*The whole world is just cause and effect*'. Exclude convention '*...and a sentient being is no different.*' That is designated as true but cannot be examined. In so far as it is examined it does not have substantial existence."

He asked, "If that is so, then who crosses over from this world to beyond this world?"

He replied, "Not even a particle of dust transfers from here to beyond this world. And yet, '*Phenomena which are void simply originate out of phenomena which are void.*' Out of the causal five void phenomena, without self and what pertains to the self, which were assigned to defilement and action, there come to originate the seven void phenomena conceived as results assigned to suffering, without self and what pertains to the self. That is its significance. It is said that these things which are without self and what pertains to the self are mutually without self and what pertains to the self. And yet phenomena essentially without self originate out of phenomena essentially without self. That should be fixed in your mind. That is the explanation."

He then asked, "What can be said by way of example about phenomena which are essentially without self originating from phenomena which are also essentially without self?"

He then replied, "Mentioning examples such as, '*In recitation, in a lamp, in a mirror, in a seal, in a rock-crystal lens, in a seed, in a tamarind, in a shout,*' clarifies both essentially not having a self and also going to another world after death.

For example the teaching of a guru transfers to the pupil but does not transfer by becoming what is not the guru's teaching. But the pupil's learning is not other than that, because then it would be occurring without having a cause. Much like the guru's teaching, a thought at the point of death does not go to another world because the fault of permanence would occur, nor is it other than in another world because the fault of lack of cause would occur. The effect of the teaching of a guru is that it becomes the learning of the pupil, but it cannot be said to be both itself and other than itself. Similarly the thought at the moment of birth is dependent on the thought at the point of death, but it cannot be said to be both itself and other than itself.

Similarly the flame of one lamp can originate from another lamp, a mirror's reflected image from your own face, an impression of a seal from a seal, fire from a rock-crystal lens, a sprout from a seed, a mouth-watering sensation from tamarind sauce and an echo from a sound. It would be rather difficult to know each of them as both itself and other than itself.

'*And even in the transmigration of the components of personal existence, the learned understand that there is no transference taking place*'. There the five components of personal existence are form, feeling, perception, mental activities and consciousness. The transmigration of these components of personal existence involves — as a result of their disappearing — their origination elsewhere, but no material particle transfers from this world to another world. Similarly the course of existence is produced by the subtle influences of false imagining. The last phrase is understood through its opposite — when it has disappeared.

Someone considering what impermanence, voidness, suffering and lack of self are, is not deluded about things. Because he is not deluded, he has no attachment. Because he has no attachment he does not become angry. Because he does not have anger he does not act. Because he does not act he does not grasp at things. Because he is not grasping he does not make existence manifest. There can be no birth from what does not exist. Mental suffering is not produced from what has not been born. So because his five causes[1] are not heaped up here no further result arises. And this itself is

1 I.e. the five components of personal existence.

release. Similarly incorrect speculations about permanence, annihilation and so on are removed.

There are two verses on this:

'But the ignorant, who imagine even the most subtle thing can come to an end,
Do not see the significance of origination from attendant causes.

There is nothing to be taken away and nothing at all to be added here;
The truth should be seen as truth and anyone who sees the truth is released.' "

* * * * *

An Interpretation of the Heart of Dependent Origination is a work completed by the noble learned teacher Nāgārjuna. It was translated and revised by: the learned Indian teacher Jinamitra, Dānaśīla, Śīlendrabodhi, the venerable Ye shes sde, et al.

Part 2

Critical study and edited Tibetan texts

Preface

The English translation of Nāgārjuna's Mahāyānaviṃśikā and his Pratītyasamutpādahṛdayakārikā with the Pratītyasamutpādahṛdayavyākhyāna — part one of this study — is complemented by part two which includes a critical study accompanied by an edited version of the Tibetan texts, the expectation being that those with only a passing interest will confine themselves to the translation alone, at least in the first instance. Later this second part may prove attractive as a contribution to the academic work available on the texts.

Twenty Verses on the Great Vehicle[1]

rgya[2] gar skad du /

ma ha' ya' na bingsha ka /

bod skad du /

theg pa chen po ni nyi shu pa[3] //

dkon mchog gsum la phyag 'tshal lo //

1 An edited version of Ānanda and Grags 'byor shes rab's translation. While reading it note the somewhat technical literalness, providing a translation not easily taken in without the help of the Sanskrit original, or at least a good knowledge of how Sanskrit functions.

Yamaguchi refers to this translation by its volume "gi", (33). Bhattacharya calls it "T*1*". Tucci follows Bhattacharya but also refers to the translations according to their order in the bstan 'gyur, i.e. T2 is "the first translation", T*1* is "the second". Therefore in Tucci's work this is the second, T*1*. In view of this variety of identification the temptation to number the versions "1" and "2" according to their order in the bstan 'gyur is best avoided. Instead, reverting to some extent to Yamaguchi's identification, volume numbers 33 (Tibetan "gi") and 17 (Tibetan "tsa") are used here. This is an attractive solution because the reference is then set by the sources themselves; indeed each folio of a Tibetan text should have the volume number printed prominently on it. Therefore where there are variant readings, comparison between an original edition of the bstan 'gyur and our editing can be made, knowing at a glance that the same volumes are being compared.

2 Bhattacharya alone has "rga". Many of his readings look like typographical errors, as this one must be.

3 Bhattacharya reads "su pa".

gang gis brjod pa'i chos kyis ni //
brjod du med kyang brtse bas bstan //
chags med blo can blo med pa'i[1] //
mthu can sangs rgyas la phyag 'tshal // [1]

skye ba don du yod ma yin //
'gag pa'ang de nyid du med de //
sangs rgyas nam[2] mkha' ji bzhin la //
sems can rnams kyang mtshan nyid gcig / [2]

pha rol tshu bzhin skyes pa yi //[3]
'dus byas[4] rten skyes de dag kyang //
rang gi ngo bo stong pa nyid //
kun mkhyen[5] ye shes spyod yul can // [3]

dngos po thams cad rang bzhin gyis //
gzugs brnyan dang ni mtshungs par 'dod //
dag[6] dang zhi[7] ba'i rang bzhin te //
gnyis med de bzhin nyid dang mtshungs // [4]

1 (N)33 "blo med pa'i", Sanskrit "acintya". (P)33 and Yamaguchi "blon med pa'i". Bhattacharya adopts "blo med pa'i", notes Yamaguchi's reading, and asks us to read "bla med pa'i", reporting "bla.med=bla.na.med".

2 Yamaguchi reads "rnam".

3 Bhattacharya implies he read "pha rol tshu rol skye med pas /" in his sNar thang Tibetan; see his p. 17 n. 2. My sNar thang agrees with the Peking and Yamaguchi, "pha rol tshul bzhin skyes pa yi //". The emendation is simply "tshu" for "tshul", as pointed out by Lindtner along with his Sanskrit reading "pārāvāram ivotpannāḥ" for Tucci's "pārāvāraṃ na cotpannaḥ". (Lindtner, Christian; Nagarjuniana : studies in the writings and philosophy of Nāgārjuna, Copenhagen, 1982, p. 12 n. 16.)

4 Misprinted as "bys" in Bhattacharya.

5 Misprinted as "mkhen" in Bhattacharya.

6 (P)33, (N)33 "bdag", but Sanskrit "śuddhāḥ" suggests "dag". Yamaguchi and Bhattacharya adopt "dag".

7 Misprinted as "zi" in Bhattacharya.

so so'i skye bo de nyid du //
bdag[1] med na yang bdag nyid du //
bde dang sdug bsngal btang snyoms dang //
nyon mongs kun tu rnam par brtag /[2] [5]

'khor bar 'gro ba rnam drug dang //
bde 'gro[3] bde ba mchog nyid dang //
dmyal bar sdug bsngal chen po dang //[4]
yul la[5] de nyid mi bsam par[6] // [6]

gzhan yang mi dge sdug bsngal dang //[7]
rga dang na[8] dang mi rtag nyid //[9]
[10]las rnams kyi ni rnam smin dang[11] //
bde ba dang ni sdug bsngal nyid //[12] [7]

1 Misprinted as "brag" in Bhattacharya.

2 The last two lines of this verse do not correspond all that well to the evidence of our Sanskrit text.

3 Lindtner convincingly suggests reading Sanskrit "ṣaḍgatayaś ca saṃsāre svarge" for Tucci's "ṣaḍgatir yaś ca saṃsāraḥ svargaś".

4 The Ngor Sanskrit manuscript omits the following. Lindtner's *haplography* theory: (his p. 12 n. 16) seems to explain the odd mix of this verse and the next verse into one verse in the Ngor manuscript.

5 (P)33, (N)33 and Bhattacharya "la". Yamaguchi omits it, causing Bhattacharya (his p. 31) to venture a complicated solution for Yamaguchi's metrically incomplete line.

6 (P)33, (N)33 and Bhattacharya "bsam par". Yamaguchi "bsams par".

7 The Ngor Sanskrit manuscript recommences with the next line.

8 Yamaguchi *corrects* this to read the more common "nad", but it is an unnecessary emendation, as Bhattacharya has pointed out in his *Notes* (p. 31).

9 Lindtner reads Sanskrit "jarāvyadhir anityatām" for Tucci's "jarāvyadhir apīyatām", based on his reported "jarāvyadhirāpībhyatām" or "jarāvyadhirapītyatām".

10 The Ngor Sanskrit manuscript omits the following.

11 (P)33, (N)33 and Bhattacharya "rnam smin dang". Yamaguchi reads "rnam par smin".

12 The Ngor Sanskrit manuscript recommences with the next line.

yang dag ri mo mkhan gyis ni //
shin tu 'jigs byed gshin rje'i[1] gzugs //
bris te rang yang 'jigs pa ltar //
'khor bar rmongs[2] pa'ang de bzhin no //[3] [8]

ji ltar rang gis 'dam byas nas //
byis pa 'ga' ba[4] 'dred pa[5] ltar //
de bzhin shin tu dka' ba yi[6] //
rnam rtog 'dam du sems can bying //[7] [9]

1 Misprinted as "gshen rje'i" in Bhattacharya. Some form of "yama" might be expected in the Sanskrit.

2 (P)33, (N)33 and Bhattacharya "rmongs". Yamaguchi reads "rmong". Some form of "saṃmūḍha" or something similar might be expected in the Sanskrit.

3 Cf. the quotation in Dharmendra's Tattvasārasaṃgraha, given below in footnote to verse 10 of Candrakumāra and Sha' kya 'od's translation of the Mahāyānaviṃśikā (p. 42).

4 (P)33, (N)33 and Yamaguchi have "dga' ba". Bhattacharya's emendation to " 'ga' ba" is supported by Sanskrit "kaścit", though if reading the Tibetan without the evidence of the Sanskrit (which in fact has: "kaścit patati baliśaḥ") Sanskrit plural rather than singular forms might have been expected.

5 (P)33, (N)33 " 'dred pa". Yamaguchi and Bhattacharya " 'dren pa".

6 (P)33, (N)33, Yamaguchi and Bhattacharya "dga' ba yi". Sanskrit "dur-", though "duruttare" may suggest consideration of some form of " 'da ba".

7 Cf. the quotation in Dharmendra's Tattvasārasaṃgraha, given below in footnote to verse 11 of Candrakumāra and Sha' kya 'od's translation of the Mahāyānaviṃśikā (p. 43).

med la yod par[1] mthong ba yis[2] //
sdug bsngal tshor ba myong bar byed //
nyam nga[3] phyin ci[4] log blo yis //
dogs[5] pa'i dug gis gnod par byed //[6] [10]

skyabs med de dag mthong nas ni //
snying rje'i dbang gyur[7] yid can gyis //
sangs rgyas phan mdzad sems can rnams //
rdzogs pa'i byang chub la sbyor[8] mdzad // [11]

de dag bsod nams tshogs bsags nas //
rtog pa'i dra ba las grol te //
ye shes bla na med pa 'thob //
sangs rgyas 'jig rten gnyen du 'gyur // [12]

1 Lindtner reads "bhāvato" for Tucci's "bhavato".

2 (P)33 and (N)33 "min". Yamaguchi emends to "yis", based upon Candrakumāra and Sha' kya 'od's translation of the text. Bhattacharya adopts "yin", based upon a reading of his sNar thang T2, i.e. Candrakumāra and Sha' kya 'od's translation of the text. The Sanskrit "abhāvaṃ bhāvato dṛṣṭvā" (following Lindtner's footnote) would not support a second negative in the phrase.

3 Suggesting perhaps Sanskrit "viṣamā" for Tucci's "viṣayā". Cf. Candrakumāra and Sha' kya 'od's verse 12 below (p. 43).

4 Misprinted as "chi" in Yamaguchi.

5 (P)33, (N)33 "dogs". Yamaguchi emends to "rtog". Bhattacharya has "rtag", but reports his sNar thang to have "rtogs" and decides in his *Notes* (p. 35) to favour Yamaguchi's emendment, stating the two readings "dogs" and "rtogs" are wrong "the true reading being *rtog*". But no emendment is necessary; "dogs" is perfectly acceptable and in accordance with Sanskrit "śaṅkā".

6 Cf. the quotation in Dharmendra's Tattvasārasaṃgraha, given below in footnote to verse 12 of Candrakumāra and Sha' kya 'od's translation of the Mahāyānaviṃśikā (p. 43).

7 Suggesting, as Lindtner points out, "adhīna" for Tucci's "dhīra". (See Lindtner's comparative references, his p. 12 n. 16.)

8 (P)33 and Yamaguchi "sbyor". (N)33 and Bhattacharya "spyod".

yang dag don ni mthong ba'i phyir //
ji bzhin ye shes skyes pa rnams //
de nas thog mtha' bar spangs pa'i //
'gro ba stong pa nyid du mthong // [13]

de dag[1] bdag nyid 'khor ba dang //
mya ngan 'das pa[2] mi mthong ngo //
ma gos 'gyur ba med pa dang //
gzod[3] nas zhi zhing 'od gsal ba'o //[4] [14]

rmi lam nyams[5] su myong ba'i yul //
sad par gyur na[6] mi mthong ngo //
rmongs pa'i mun pa sad pa yis //
'khor ba mthong ba ma yin nyid // [15]

1 Lindtner reads Sanskrit "te na" for Tucci's "tena". Presumably Tucci was following Candrakumāra and Sha' kya 'od's "de ltar". Cf. their verse 16 below (p. 44).
2 Misprinted as " 'das pa'i" in Yamaguchi.
3 Misprinted as "gzong" in Bhattacharya.
4 Tucci's Sanskrit has "ādimadhyāntabhāsvaram". Cf. Candrakumāra and Sha' kya 'od's verse 16 below (p. 44). For the Tibetan above Bhattacharya's reconstructed Sanskrit "ādiśāntaṃ prabhāsvaram" (his p. 12) serves well, though in fact it cannot relate to any manuscript evidence.
5 Misprinted as "ngams" in Bhattacharya.
6 (P)33, (N)33 and Yamaguchi "na". Bhattacharya emends to "ni" against all readings. It should be borne in mind however that his main Tibetan source is a copy of the sNar thang edition, an edition where loss of an expected "gi gu" is so common that modern editors would not be expected to point it out. Its printing of vowels above the line can be remarkably haphazard.

rang bzhin med pa'i dngos rnams la //
rtag bdag bde ba'i[1] 'du shes kyis //
chags[2] rmongs mun pas bsgribs pa na[3] //
srid pa'i rgya[4] mtsho 'di 'byung ngo // [16]

skye ba[5] rang nyid ma skyes[6] rnams //
'jig rten rnams kyis skye bar brtags //
rnam par rtog dang sems[7] can rnams //
'di dag[8] gnyis kar rig[9] ma yin //[10] [17]

1 (P)33 and (N)33 "med pa'i". Yamaguchi "bde ba'i". It is worth considering how similar the two can look in Tibetan script. Bhattacharya follows Yamaguchi against his reported sNar thang "med". Tucci's Sanskrit "sukha" supports "bde ba'i". Cf. Candrakumāra and Sha' kya 'od's verse 21 below (p. 46).

2 Tucci's Sanskrit has "bālā", not "rāga". Cf. "byis pa" in Candrakumāra and Sha' kya 'od's verse 21 below (p. 46).

3 (N)33 and Bhattacharya "na". (P)33 and Yamaguchi "ni".

4 Misprinted as "rga" in Bhattacharya.

5 (P)33, (N)33 and Yamaguchi "skye ba". Bhattacharya "skye bo" as his emendment for "skye ba".

6 (P)33, (N)33 and Bhattacharya "skyes". Yamaguchi has "skye".

7 Misprinted as "sesm" in Yamaguchi, as Bhattacharya has pointed out.

8 (P)33, (N)33 and Yamaguchi "dag". Bhattacharya reads "dang".

9 (P)33, (N)33 "rig". Yamaguchi and Bhattacharya (against his sNar thang reading) have "rigs".

10 This verse does not match the Sanskrit particularly well. Its "sems can rnams" would suggest a plural form of "sattva" but none is to be found. Almost everything appears in the plural in the Tibetan here while the Sanskrit has an assortment of singulars for the most part.

'di dag thams cad sems tsam ste[1] //
sgyu mar 'gyur ba bzhin du skye //[2]
de las dge dang mi dge las //
de las skye ba bzang[3] dang ngan //[4] [18]

sems kyi 'khor ba[5] 'gags pa na //
kun gyi chos nyid 'gag pa yin //
de nyid chos la bdag med de //
de nyid chos kyi rnam dag ste //[6] [19]

1 (P)33, (N)33 and Bhattacharya "ste". Yamaguchi "te".
2 Lindtner's suggestion "perhaps māyākārasamutthitam" provides an alternative to Tucci's Sanskrit "māyākāravad utthitam".
3 Misprinted as "ske ba bzhang" in Bhattacharya.
4 Cf. the quotation of this verse cited as being Nāgārjuna's in Āryadeva's Caryāmelāyanapradīpa (Peking bstan 'gyur — rgyud 'grel 33 (gi) 95a3–95a4):

> " 'di dag thams cad sems tsam ste //
> sgyu ma'i rnam par yang dag 'byung //
> de nas dge dang mi dge'i las //
> des ni bde 'gro ngan 'gror skye //"

5 Note " 'khor lo", suggesting Sanskrit "cakra" and not "saṃsāra" below in verse 20 of Candrakumāra and Sha' kya 'od's translation of the Mahāyānaviṃśikā (p. 45).
6 Note the play on words in this verse as "chos" (Sanskrit "dharma") is repeated three times, i.e. "kun gyi chos nyid" "the essence of all dharmas", "de nyid chos la" "in the true nature of dharmas", "de nyid chos kyi" "of the true nature of dharmas". The meaning of "dharma" is wide enough to cover "phenomena" as well as to imply the sense of dharma as "teaching", the purity of the true nature of things or the purity of the true nature of the teachings.

* * * * * * *[1]
theg pa che la ma brten par[2] //
'khor ba'i rgya[3] mtsho chen po yi //
pha rol brgal bar 'gyur ba min[4] //[5] [20]

theg pa chen po nyi shu[6] pa slob dpon 'phags pa klu sgrub kyis mdzad pa rdzogs so // kha che'i paṇḍi ta a' nanda dang / lo tsa'[7] ba dge slong grags 'byor shes rab kyis bsgyur ba'o[8] //

1 (P)33 and (N)33 have a line missing here. Bhattacharya marks the missing line with stars and Yamaguchi marks the missing line with tshegs. As sources providing the general sense of this verse are plentiful it takes little imagination to be able to fill in the sense of this missing line.
2 (P)33, (N)33 and Bhattacharya "brten par". Yamaguchi "rten par".
3 Misprinted as "rga" in Bhattacharya.
4 (P)33, (N)33 and Yamaguchi "min". Bhattacharya "med".
5 Cf. the quotation in Dharmendra's Tattvasārasaṃgraha, given below in footnote to verse 22 of Candrakumāra and Sha' kya 'od's translation of the Mahāyānaviṃśikā (p. 46).
6 (P)33, (N)33 "shu". Yamaguchi has "zhu". Bhattacharya has "su".
7 (P)33, (N)33 and Yamaguchi "tsa'". Bhattacharya "tsa".
8 (P)33, (N)33 and Bhattacharya "ba'o". Yamaguchi "bo".

Twenty Verses on the Great Vehicle[1]

rgya gar skad du /

ma ha' ya'[2] na biṃ shi ka'[3] /

bod skad du /

theg pa chen po nyi shu pa //

'jam dpal gzhon nur gyur pa la phyag 'tshal lo //

1 An edited version of Candrakumāra and Sha' kya 'od's translation. While reading it notice the somewhat interpretative style, providing a translation easily taken in without the help of the Sanskrit original. Its readable style makes it by far the more accessible Tibetan translation.

Yamaguchi refers to this translation by its volume "tsa". Bhattacharya calls it "T2". Tucci follows Bhattacharya but also refers to it as "the first translation". Our references are to the volume number 17 (Tibetan "tsa"), cf. p. 29 above.

2 (D)17, (C)17 "ya'". (P)17, (N)17 "ya".

3 (D)17, (C)17 "biṃ shi ka'". (P)17 "bingsha ki'". (N)17 "bing ki'".

chags med thugs su chud sangs rgyas //
rjod byed brjod par bya ba min //
thugs rjes rgyal ba[1] snang gyur pa //
mthu bsam mi khyab phyag 'tshal lo // [1]

dam pa'i don du[2] skye med phyir //
de nyid du ni grol ba'ang med //
mkha' bzhin sangs rgyas de bzhin te //
sems can dang ni mtshan nyid gcig[3] / [2]

pha rol tshu[4] rol skye med pas //
rang bzhin mya ngan 'das pa'ang med //[5]
de bzhin 'dus byas[6] mngon par stong //
kun mkhyen ye shes spyod yul yin // [3]

dngos po kun gyi rang bzhin ni[7] //
gzugs brnyan dang ni mtshungs par rtogs //
rnam dag zhi ba'i[8] ngo bo nyid //
gnyis med de bzhin nyid du mnyam // [4]

bdag dang bdag med bden min te //
so so'i skye bos brtags pa yin //
bde dang sdug bsngal ltos pa[9] ste //
nyon mongs rnams dang grol de bzhin //[10] [5]

1 Here "rgyal ba" would have to correspond to Sanskrit "dharmaḥ" on the evidence of our Sanskrit text. Was Candrakumāra and Sha' kya 'od's Sanskrit source quite different?

2 Here "dam pa'i don du" would have to correspond to Sanskrit "svabhāvena" on the evidence of our Sanskrit text.

3 (D)17, (C)17 "gcig". (P)17, (N)17, Yamaguchi and Bhattacharya "cig".

4 (N)17, (D)17, (C)17, Yamaguchi and Bhattacharya "tshu". (P)17 "tshul". Cf. Ānanda and Grags 'byor shes rab's verse 3 (p. 30) above.

5 This line is a good example of one which does not correspond to the evidence of our Sanskrit text.

6 (P)17, (N)17, (D)17, Yamaguchi and Bhattacharya "byas". (C)17 "gyis".

7 (P)17, (N)17, Yamaguchi and Bhattacharya "ni". (D)17, (C)17 "no".

8 (P)17, (N)17, (D)17, Yamaguchi and Bhattacharya "zhi ba'i". (C)17 "ri ba'i".

9 (P)17, (N)17, (D)17, (C)17 and Yamaguchi "ltos pa". Bhattacharya adopts this but reports his sNar thang to have "bltos pa". In his *Notes*, if the positions of T2c and T*1*c are reversed then the sentence found under *Restoration* makes some sense, (his p. 30).

10 The last two lines of this verse do not correspond to the evidence of our Sanskrit text.

'gro ba rigs[1] drug 'khor ba ru[2] //
mtho ris[3] mchog dang bde ba dang //
dmyal bar sdug bsngal chen po[4] ste //[5]
de dag yul rnams nyams su myong[6] // [6]

mi dges mchog tu sdug bsngal zhing //
dga' na mi rtag rgud pa[7] yin //
dge ba'i las rnams nyid kyis kyang //
bzang po nyid du nges pa yin //[8] [7]

skye med rtog pas[9] bskrun pa yis //
dmyal la sogs pa snang ba ni //
nyes pa nags kyi[10] me bzhin bsreg /[11]
* * * * * * * [12] [8]

1 (P)17, (D)17, (C)17, Yamaguchi and Bhattacharya "rigs". (N)17 "rig". (P)17 has the "sa" added below the "ga", looking rather like an after thought.

2 (P)17, (N)17, (D)17, Yamaguchi and Bhattacharya "ru". (C)17 "du".

3 Lindtner convincingly suggests reading Sanskrit "ṣaḍgatayaś ca saṃsāre svarge" for Tucci's "ṣaḍgatir yaś ca saṃsāraḥ svargaś" as mentioned before (see footnote to Ānanda and Grags 'byor shes rab's verse 6 (p. 31 above).

4 (P)17, (N)17, (D)17, Yamaguchi and Bhattacharya "chen po". (C)17 "zhen pa".

5 Lindtner's *haplography* theory (his p. 12 n. 16) seems to explain the odd mix of this verse and the next verse into one verse in the Ngor Sanskrit manuscript. Ānanda and Grags 'byor shes rab's Tibetan translation more clearly supports the theory, cf. footnote 4 (p. 31 above) and their verses 6 and 7.

6 (P)17, (N)17, (D)17, Yamaguchi and Bhattacharya "su myong". (C)17 may be "su myong" with its "zhabs kyu" missing, but it is very unclear.

7 (P)17, (N)17, (D)17, Yamaguchi and Bhattacharya "rgud pa". C(17) "dud pa", but these lines are very unclear in the Co ne edition.

8 Cf. Ānanda and Grags 'byor shes rab's strikingly different verse 7 (p. 31) above.

9 (P)17, (N)17, (D)17, (C)17 and Bhattacharya "rtogs pas". Yamaguchi agrees with this reading but emends it to "rtog pas", and Bhattacharya accepts this in his *Notes*, expecting a form of "kalpanā" in the Sanskrit. The Sanskrit turns out to be "kalpanāṃ" supporting the emendment.

10 The Sanskrit has "veṇavo", "bamboo".

11 This line equals two pādas of the Sanskrit instead of the expected one. Probably "nyes pa" ("svadoṣeṇaiva") once had a line of its own. Both Yamaguchi and Bhattacharya report the second line of the verse to be missing, not the fourth line. The Chinese and the Sanskrit of the Ngor manuscript are complete.

12 (P)17, (N)17, (D)17 and (C)17 have a line missing here, in the sense that there is no fourth line in the verse, as explained in the preceding footnote. Bhattacharya marks the second line of the verse as missing, with stars and Yamaguchi marks the second line of the verse as missing, with tshegs.

sgyu ma ji lta ji lta bar //
de bzhin sems can yul la spyod //
'gro ba sgyu ma'i rang bzhin yin //
de bzhin du ni brten nas byung //[1] [9]

ji ltar ri mo mkhan gyis[2] gzugs //
gnod sbyin 'jigs pa bris pa yis //
de yis rang nyid skrag pa[3] ltar //
mi mkhas[4] 'khor bar de bzhin no //[5] [10]

ji ltar rang gis 'dam g.yos pas //
byis pa 'ga' zhig bying ba ltar //

Cf. the quotation of this verse cited as being from Nāgārjuna's Mahāyānaviṃśikā in Dharmendra's Tattvasārasaṃgraha (Peking bstan 'gyur — rgyud 'grel 72 (nu) 100a5):

"yang dag ma yin rtog byas pas //
dmyal la sogs par bsregs 'gyur te //
'od ma yi ni me bzhin du //
rang gi nyes pas sreg par byed //"

1 Cf. the quotation of this verse cited as being from Nāgārjuna's Mahāyānaviṃśikā in Dharmendra's Tattvasārasaṃgraha (Peking bstan 'gyur — rgyud 'grel 72 (nu) 100a5–100a6):

"sems can sgyu ma ji bzhin du //
yul ni yongs su spyod par byed //
de bzhin rten 'brel las byung ba //
sgyu ma'i rang bzhin bgrod par 'gro //"

2 (D)17, (C)17 and Yamaguchi "gyis". (P)17, (N)17 "gyi". Bhattacharya adopts Yamaguchi's "gyis" but reports sNar thang "gyi".

3 (N)17, (D)17, (C)17 and Bhattacharya "skrag pa". (P)17 and Yamaguchi "sgrag pa".

4 Supporting the Sanskrit "abudhas". Cf. Ānanda and Grags 'byor shes rab's verse 8 (p. 32) above, both for this and for variations in the verse as a whole.

5 Cf. the quotation of this verse cited as being from Nāgārjuna's Mahāyānaviṃśikā in Dharmendra's Tattvasārasaṃgraha (Peking bstan 'gyur — rgyud 'grel 72 (nu) 100a6–100a7):

"dper na ri mo mkhan gyis ni //
gnod sbyin gzugs ni rab 'jigs pa //
bris nas rang nyid 'jigs pa ltar //
'khor bar mi mkhas de dang mtshungs //"

de bzhin rtog pa'i[1] 'dam bying bas //
sems can rnams ni 'byung mi nus //[2] [11]

dngos med dngos por lta ba yis[3] //
sdug bsgnal tshor ba nyams su myong //
yul[4] dang shes pa de dag tu //
rnam par rtog pa'i[5] dug gis bcings //[6] [12]

de dag snying po med mthong bas //
shes rab snying rje'i yid kyis ni //
sems can rnams la phan pa'i phyir //
rdzogs sangs rgyas la sbyar bar[7] bya // [13]

1 (D)17, (C)17, Yamaguchi and Bhattacharya "rtog pa'i". (P)17, (N)17 "rtogs pa'i".

2 Cf. the quotation of this verse cited as being from Nāgārjuna's Mahāyānaviṃśikā in Dharmendra's Tattvasārasaṃgraha (Peking bstan 'gyur — rgyud 'grel 72 (nu) 100a7–100a8):

> "ji ltar byis pa rang gis 'dam //
> byas nas la la ldud bar byed //
> de bzhin kun tu rtog pa'i 'dam //
> dgrol dkar sems can bying ba dang //"

3 (P)17, (N)17, (D)17, (C)17 and Yamaguchi "yis". Yamaguchi based his "yis" in editing Ānanda and Grags 'byor shes rab's translation on this occurrence. Bhattacharya accepts "yis" here but reports "N *yin*". He justifies adopting "yin" in his T1 because of this occurrence in his T2, cf. Ānanda and Grags 'byor shes rab's verse 10 (p. 33) above.

4 This presumably contributed to Tucci's reading of Sanskrit "viṣayā". Cf. Ānanda and Grags 'byor shes rab's verse 10 (p. 33) above.

5 (D)17, (C)17 and Yamaguchi "rtog pa'i". Bhattacharya follows Yamaguchi but notes "N *rtog*". (P)17, (N)17 "rtogs pa'i".

6 Cf. the quotation of this verse cited as being from Nāgārjuna's Mahāyānaviṃśikā in Dharmendra's Tattvasārasaṃgraha (Peking bstan 'gyur — rgyud 'grel 72 (nu) 100a8–100b1):

> "dngos med dngos por mthong nas ni //
> sdug bsngal sna tshogs myod 'gyur te //
> log pa'i bsam ba las byung bas //
> rtog pa'i dug gis 'chi bar 'gyur //"
> (i.e. 'ching bar 'gyur)

7 (P)17, (N)17, (D)17, (C)17 "sbyar bar" Yamaguchi "sbyor bar".

des kyang tshogs bsags kun rdzob tu //
bla na med pa'i byang chub thob //
rtog pa'i 'ching ba rnams las grol //
sangs rgyas de ni 'jig rten gnyen // [14]

ji ltar rten cing 'brel 'byung ba //
gang gis yang dag don du gzigs //
de yis 'gro ba stong par mkhyen //
thog ma dbus dang tha ma spangs // [15]

de ltar[1] mthong bas 'khor ba dang //
mya ngan 'das pa'ang de nyid min //
nyon mongs pa yi rnam pa med //
thog ma dbus mtha'i rang bzhin bsal[2] //[3] [16]

rmi lam nyams su[4] myong ba bzhin //
so sor rtog pas snang ma yin[5] //
rmongs pa'i mun pa gnyid sad la //
'khor ba rnams ni dmigs pa med // [17]

1 Lindtner reads Sanskrit "te na" for Tucci's "tena" as mentioned before (cf. footnote to Ānanda and Grags 'byor shes rab's verse 14 (p. 34) above).

2 (P)17, (N)17, (D)17, (C)17 and Yamaguchi "bsal". Bhattacharya "gsal".

3 As Yamaguchi pointed out (his p. 175), this repetition of the content of the last line of the preceding verse suggests, "There must have been some confusion." It is not the complete line which is repeated here; Yamaguchi overstated the case. The Sanskrit is "ādimadhyāntabhāsvaram" as mentioned before, (see footnote to Ānanda and Grags 'byor shes rab's verse 14 (p. 34) above).

4 Misprinted as "sa" in Bhattacharya.

5 (D)17 "so sor rtog pas snang ma yin". (C)17 "so sor rtogs pas snang ma yin". (P)17, (N)17 "so sor rtog pas snang ba yin". Yamaguchi and Bhattacharya "so sor rtogs pas snang ba min", based on Yamaguchi's emendment of his reading "so sor rtog pas snang ba yin".

sgyu mas sprul pa[1] sgyu mar mthong //
gang tshe 'dus pa de yi[2] tshe //
cung zad yod pa ma yin te //
de ni chos rnams chos nyid yin //[3] [18]

'di dag thams cad sems tsam ste[4] //
sgyu ma lta bur gnas pa yin //[5]
dge dang mi dge las rnams kyis //
de yis bzang ngan skye ba rnams //[6] [19]

sems kyi 'khor lo 'gags pa yis //
chos rnams thams cad 'gag pa nyid //
de phyir chos nyid bdag med cing //
des na chos nyid rnam par dag / [20]

1 Lindtner reads Sanskrit "māyāvī" for Tucci's "māyavī", a suggestion which provides a better spelling and also fits the metre.

2 (D)17 "de yi", misprinted as "de li" in (C)17. (P)17, (N)17 "de'i", against the metre.

3 Cf. the quotation of this verse cited as being from Nāgārjuna's Mahāyānaviṃśikā in Dharmendra's Tattvasārasaṃgraha (Peking bstan 'gyur — rgyud 'grel 72 (nu) 100a6):

> "gang tshe sgyu mkhan sgyu ma yi //
> spangs shing nye bar bsdus pa na //
> de tshe ci yang mi snang ste //
> de ni chos kyi chos nyid yin //"

4 (D)17, (C)17 "ste". (P)17, (N)17, Yamaguchi and Bhattacharya "te". Bhattacharya also reports sNar thang "can te".

5 Lindtner's suggestion "perhaps māyākārasamutthitam" provides an alternative to Tucci's Sanskrit "māyākāravad utthitam" as mentioned before (see footnote to Ānanda and Grags 'byor shes rab's verse 18 (p. 36) above).

6 Cf. the quotation in Āryadeva's Caryāmelāyanapradīpa, given above in footnote to verse 18 of Ānanda and Grags 'byor shes rab's translation of the Mahāyānaviṃśikā (p. 36).

dngos po 'am ni rang bzhin la //
rtag tu bde bar 'du shes shing //
rmongs pa'i mun pas bsgribs pa[1] na //
byis pa[2] 'khor ba'i rgya mtshor 'khyam[3] // [21]

rtog pa'i chu bos gang ba yi //
'khor ba'i rgya mtsho chen po la //
theg chen gru la mi zhon pa[4] //
gang gis pha rol phyin par 'gyur //[5] [22]

ma rig[6] rkyen gyis byung ba 'di //
yang dag 'jig rten mkhyen pa'i phyir //
rnam par rtog pa 'di dag ni //
ci zhig las ni 'byung bar 'gyur // [23]

theg pa chen po nyi shu pa slob dpon klu sgrub kyi zhal snga nas mdzad pa rdzogs so[7] // // rgya gar gyi mkhan po tsandra ku ma' ra[8] dang / dge slong sha' kya 'od kyis bsgyur[9] ba'o[10] //

1 (D)17, (C)17 "pa". (P)17, (N)17, Yamaguchi and Bhattacharya "pas".
2 Tucci's Sanskrit has "bālā" as mentioned before (see footnote to Ānanda and Grags 'byor shes rab's verse 16 (p. 35 above).
3 Tucci's Sanskrit has "bhramanti", translated by " 'khyam" here, which is preferable to Ānanda and Grags 'byor shes rab's " 'byung".
4 (P)17, (D)17, (C)17, Yamaguchi "zhon pa". (N)17 and Bhattacharya "zhon par".
5 Cf. the quotation of this verse cited as being from Nāgārjuna's Mahāyānaviṃśikā in Dharmendra's Tattvasārasaṃgraha (Peking bstan 'gyur — rgyud 'grel 72 (nu) 92a7):

"rtog pa 'i chu yis gang ba yi //
'khor ba'i rgya mtsho chen por ni //
theg chen gru la ma zhugs par //
su zhig pha rol 'gro bar 'gyur //"

6 (P)17, (D)17, (C)17, Yamaguchi and Bhattacharya "rig". (N)17 "rigs". (Bhattacharya reports sNar thang "rigs".)
7 Misprinted as "s.ho" in (P)17, (i.e. "ha" with a "sa" head and "na ro".)
8 (D)17, (C)17 "tsandra ku ma' ra". (P)17, (N)17, Yamaguchi "tsan dra ku ma ra". Bhattacharya reads "tsan dra ku ma' ra".
9 Misprinted as "bsgur" in Bhattacharya.
10 (D)17, (C)17 "ba'o". (P)17, (N)17, Yamaguchi and Bhattacharya omit it.

Verses on the Heart of Dependent Origination[1]

rgya gar skad du /

pra ti'[2] tya sa mu tpa'[3] da hri[4] da ya

ka' ri ka' /

bod skad du /

rten cing 'brel bar 'byung ba'i snying po'i

tshig le'ur byas pa /

'jam dpal gzhon nur gyur pa la phyag 'tshal lo //

1 The volume numbers 17 (Tibetan "tsa") and 33 (Tibetan "gi") provide versions of this text similar enough to be presented as one edition. Cf. p. 29 above.

2 (P)33, (N)33 "ti'". (P)17, (N)17, (D)17, (C)17 "ti".

3 (P)17, (P)33, (N)17, (N)33 "tpa'". (D)17, (C)17 "tpa".

4 (N)33 "hri". (P)17, (P)33, (N)17, (D)17, (C)17 "hrī".

yan lag bye brag bcu gnyis gang //
thub pas rten 'byung gsungs de dag /
nyon mongs las dang sdug bsngal dang //
gsum po dag tu zad par 'dus // [1]

dang po brgyad dang dgu nyon mongs //
gnyis dang bcu pa las yin te //
lhag ma bdun yang sdug bsngal yin[1] //
bcu gnyis chos ni gsum du 'dus //[2] [2]

gsum po dag las gnyis 'byung ste //
gnyis las bdun 'byung bdun las kyang //
gsum 'byung srid pa'i 'khor lo de[3] //
nyid[4] ni yang dang yang du[5] 'khor //[6] [3]

1 (P)33, (N)17, (N)33, (D)17, (C)17 "yin". (P)17 "yan". La Vallée Poussin reads "yang".

2 Cf. the identical quotation of this verse in Bhavya's Madhyamakaratnapradīpa (Peking bstan 'gyur — mdo 'grel 17 (tsha) 342a3).

3 (P)17, (N)17, (D)17, (C)17 "de". (P)33, (N)33 "ste".

4 (P)17, (N)17, (D)17, (C)17 "nyid". (P)33, (N)33 " 'di".

5 (P)17, (P)33, (N)17, (N)33, (D)17, (C)17 "yang du". La Vallée Poussin reads "du yang".

6 Cf. the truncated quotation of this verse in Bhavya's Madhyamakaratnapradīpa (Peking bstan 'gyur — mdo 'grel 17 (tsha) 342a3–342a4):

> "gsum las gnyis 'byung gnyis las kyang //
> bdun 'byung * * * * *
> * * srid pa'i 'khor lo ni //
> yang dang yang du 'jug par 'gyur //

'gro kun rgyu dang 'bras bu ste //
'di la[1] sems can gzhan ci'ang[2] med //
stong pa kho na'i chos rnams las //
stong pa'i chos rnams 'byung bar[3] zad //[4] [4]

1 (P)17, (N)17, (D)17, (C)17 "la". (P)33, (N)33 "las".

2 (P)33, (N)33 "gzhan ci'ang". (P)17, (N)17, (D)17, (C)17 "ci yang" on its own. La Vallée Poussin and Lindtner also read "ci yang" on its own. Bhavya's Madhyamakaratnapradīpa quotation has "gzhan ci'ang". Gokhale reads Sanskrit "anyo" along with "kaścid".

3 (P)33, (N)33 " 'byung bar". (P)17, (N)17, (D)17, (C)17 " 'byung ba". Lindtner adopts " 'byung ba".

4 Cf. the quotation of this verse in Bhavya's Madhyamakaratnapradīpa (Peking bstan 'gyur — mdo 'grel 17 (tsha) 342a4–342a5):

" 'gro kun rgyu dang 'bras bu ste //
'di na sems can gzhan ci'ang med //
stong pa kho na'i chos rnams las //
stong pa kho na 'byung bar 'gyur //

The second half of this verse is quoted twice in Prajñākaramati's Bodhicaryāvatārapañjikā, see La Vallée Poussin's Bodhicaryāvatārapañjikā, Prajñākaramati's Commentary to the Bodhicaryāvatāra of Çāntideva, Calcutta, 1901–1914, p. 355.14 and 532.5. It is also quoted in Kambalapāda's Navaślokī, see Tucci's Navaślokī of Kambalapāda, p. 229 n. 1, (Section III) in his Minor Buddhist texts, Roma, 1956.

(D)17 and (C)17 follow the final line of this verse with "bdag dang bdag gi med pa'i chos //". Even though it fits the metre it is out of place and does not fit the pattern of four line verses. (P)17, (P)33, (N)17 and (N)33 omit it. It is found as the next phrase following this verse in the Pratītyasamutpādahṛdayavyākhyāna and might suggest that the Pratītyasamutpādahṛdayakārikā here was constructed from the verses of its commentary, the Pratītyasamutpādahṛdayavyākhyāna.

kha ton[1] mar me me long rgya[2] //
me shel[3] sa bon skyur[4] dang sgras //
phung po nying mtshams sbyor ba yang //
mi 'pho bar yang mkhas rtogs bya //[5] [5]

1 (P)17, (P)33, (N)17, (N)33 "ton". (D)17, (C)17 "thon".

2 (P)33, (N)33, (D)17, (C)17 "rgya". (P)17, (N)17 "brgya". La Vallée Poussin reads "brgya".

3 The Sanskrit "arkakānta" in its sense as "a rock-crystal lens", having much the same effect as a magnifying glass used to start a fire, is not often found in dictionaries. The object in mind would be rock-crystal cut into a convex shape and used as a burning lens. La Vallée Poussin took the Tibetan to mean "la pierre de soleil" ("sunstone", "quartz"). Aiyaswami Sastri took the Chinese to mean "spark". Cf. Sanskrit "sūryakānta".

4 The Tibetan may suggest nothing more than something sour and if a specific plant comes to mind it would probably be myrobalan, but the Sanskrit "amla" might suggest "tamarind" ("amla-phala").

5 Cf. the prose quotation of this verse in Bhavya's Prajñāpradīpa (Peking bstan 'gyur — mdo 'grel 17 (tsha) 314a6–314a7):

"...kha dog dang / mar me dang rgya dang / me long dang / skad dang / me shel dang / sa bon dang / sgyur dag gis phung po'i nying mtshams sbyor ba mi 'pho bar mkhas pa rnams kyis rtogs par bya'o zhes zer ro // "

Also cf. the quotation of this verse in Bhavya's Madhyamakaratnapradīpa (Peking bstan 'gyur — mdo 'grel 17 (tsha) 342a5):

"kha ton me long mar me rgya //
me shel skyur dang sa bon sgras //
phung po nying mtshams sbyor ba ni //
mi 'pho bar yang mkhas rtogs bya //"

This verse is also quoted twice in Candrakīrti's Prasannapadā Madhyamakavṛtti, see La Vallée Poussin's Madhyamakavṛttiḥ, Mūlamadhyamakakārikās (Mādhyamikasūtras) de Nāgārjuna avec la Prasannapadā commentaire de Candrakīrti, St.-Pétersbourg, 1903–1913, p. 428.11 and 551.14.

shin tu phra ba'i dngos la[1] yang //
gang gis[2] chad par rnam brtags pa[3] //
rnam par mi mkhas de yis[4] ni //
rkyen las 'byung ba'i[5] don ma mthong //[6] [6]

1 (P)17, (P)33, (N)33, (D)17, (C)17 "la". (N)17 "la la".
2 (P)17, (P)33, (N)17, (N)33 "gis". (D)17, (C)17 "gi".
3 (P)33, (N)17, (N)33, (D)17, (C)17 "brtags pa". (P)17 "rtags pa". La Vallée Poussin reads "rtags pa".
4 (P)17, (P)33, (N)17, (N)33 "yis". (D)17, (C)17 "yi".
5 (P)17, (P)33, (N)17, (N)33, (D)17, (C)17 "rkyen las byung ba'i". La Vallée Poussin reads "rkyen la 'byung ba'i". Lindtner reads "rkyen las skyes pa'i".
6 Cf. the strikingly similar verse 12 of Nāgārjuna's Yuktiṣaṣṭikākārikā:

> "dngos po shin tu phra ba la'ang //
> gang gis skye bar rnam brtags pa //
> rnam par mi mkhas de yis ni //
> rkyen las byung ba'i don ma mthong //

(Schaeffer, Philipp; Yukti-ṣaṣṭikā : die 60 Sätze des Negativismus nach der chinesischen Version übersetzt, Heidelberg, 1923, 23a4–23a5 of the second photograph of the first page of facsimiles. Also cf. Lindtner, Christian; Nagarjuniana, p. 106 f. The canonical reference to the Peking edition which Schaeffer used would be: Nāgārjuna's Yuktiṣaṣṭikākārikā (i.e. Rigs pa drug cu pa'i tshig le'ur byas pa). Peking bstan 'gyur — mdo 'grel 17 (tsha) 23a4–23a5.)

Also cf. the virtually identical quotation of this verse in Bhavya's Madhyamakaratnapradīpa (Peking bstan 'gyur — mdo 'grel 17 (tsha) 342a5–342a6):

> "shin tu phra ba'i dngos la yang //
> gang gis chad par rnam brtags pa //
> rnam par mi mkhas de yis ni //
> rkyen las byung ba'i don ma mthong //

'di la bsal[1] bya gang yang med //
gzhag par[2] bya ba ci yang med //
yang dag nyid la yang dag blta //
yang dag mthong na[3] rnam par grol //[4] [7]

rten cing 'brel par 'byung ba'i snying po'i tshig le'ur byas pa // slob dpon 'phags pa klu sgrub kyis mdzad pa rdzogs so // //

1 (P)17, (P)33, (N)17 "bsal". (N)33, (D)17, (C)17 "gsal".
2 (P)17, (D)17, (C)17 "gzhag par". (P)33, (N)17, (N)33 "bzhag par".
3 (P)17, (N)17, (D)17, (C)17 "na". (P)33, (N)33 "nas". La Vallée Poussin reads "na".
4 This is what Jikido Takasaki refers to as "one of the most famous verses in Mahāyānistic literature." For the first stages of a list of occurrences combine Takasaki, Jikido; A study on the Ratnagotravibhāga, Roma, 1966, p. 300 f. (including and supplementing what is found in La Vallée Poussin, Louis de; Notes et bibliographie bouddhiques, *Mélanges chinois et bouddhiques*, Paris : 1932; 1: 394) with Lindtner, Christian; Adversaria Buddhica, *WZKS*, Wien : 1982; 26: 168 n. 4. Flemming Faber traces the verse in the dMyigs su med pa tshul gcig pa'i gzung (Pelliot 116) and in Vimalamitra's Cig car 'jug pa rnam par mi rtog pa'i bsgom don (see his: A Tibetan Dunhuang treatise on simultaneous enlightenment: the *dMyigs su myed pa tshul gcig pa' i gzhung*, *Acta Orientalia*, Copenhagen : 1985; 46: 71–72). The verse is also found in gNubs chen Sangs rgyas ye shes' bSam gtan mig sgron. (See: gNubs-chen Saṅs-rgyas-ye-śes; Rnal 'byor mig gi bsam gtan or Bsam gtan mig gron : a treatise on bhāvanā and dhyāna and the relationships between the various approaches to Buddhist contemplative practice, Leh, 1974, 23b6–24a2. This is commented upon in David Seyfort Ruegg's *Buddha-nature, mind and the problem of gradualism in a comparative perspective*, London, 1989, p. 85.)

An Interpretation of the Heart of Dependent Origination[1]

rgya gar skad du /

pra ti'[2] tya sa mu tpa'[3] da hri[4] da ya bya'[5] khya na /

bod skad du /

rten cing 'brel par 'byung ba'i snying po'i rnam par bshad pa /

'jam dpal gzhon nur gyur pa la phyag 'tshal lo //

1 The volume numbers 17 (Tibetan "tsa") and 33 (Tibetan "gi") provide versions of this text similar enough to be presented as one edition. Cf. p. 29 above. Sanskrit references are to Gokhale's 1968 edition.

2 (P)33, (N)33 "ti'". (P)17, (N)17, (D)17, (C)17 "ti".

3 (P)17, (P)33, (N)17, (N)33 "tpa'". (D)17, (C)17 "tpa".

4 (P)17, (P)33, (N)17, (C)17 "hri". (D)17, (N)33 "hrī".

5 (D)17, (C)17 "bya'". (P)17, (P)33, (N)17, (N)33 "bya".

'di la dge sbyong nyan 'dod pa[1] mnyan pa dang / gzung ba dang / khong du chud par bya ba dang / rtog pa dang /[2] sel nus pa dang ldan pa'i slob ma zhig slob dpon gyi gan du[3] 'ongs nas / de bzhin gshegs pa'i[4] bstan pa las[5] brtsams te /[6] 'di skad 'dri'o // bcom ldan 'das 'di la / *yan lag bye brag*[7] *bcu gnyis gang // thub pas rten 'byung gsungs de dag /*[8] gang du bsdu bar[9] blta ba[10] thos par 'tshal lo //

de[11] chos de dag gi[12] de kho na nyid 'dri bar rig nas / slob dpon gyis[13] 'di skad ces bu[14] / *nyon mongs las dang sdug bsngal dang // gsum po dag tu zad par 'dus //*

zhes[15] gsal zhing zur phyin pa'i tshig 'di[16] smras so // de la bcu dang gnyis ni bcu gnyis so // yan lag rnams[17] nyid bye brag yin pas na[18] yan lag bye brag ste / shing rta'i yan lag bzhin du yan lag tu gyur pa[19] bstan to // sku dang gsung dang thugs[20] thub pas na[21] thub pa'o //[22] thub pa des

1 (P)17, (N)17, (D)17, (C)17 " 'dod pa /". (P)33, (N)33 " 'dod pas".
2 (P)17, (N)17, (D)17, (C)17 "dang /". (P)33 and (N)33 omit it.
3 (N)17, (D)17, (C)17 "gan du". (P)17, (P)33, (N)33 "gam du".
4 (P)33, (N)33 "de bzhin gshegs pa'i". (P)17, (N)17, (D)17, (C)17 "de bzhin gshegs pas".
5 (P)33, (N)33, (D)17, (C)17 "las". (P)17, (N)17 "la".
6 The Tibetan alone would suggest that it is the pupil beginning in the Tathāgata's teachings, but the Sanskrit case endings suggest it must be the teacher beginning his explanation of the Tathāgata's doctrine.
7 (P)33, (N)17, (N)33, (D)17, (C)17 "*bye brag*". (P)17 "*bya brag*".
8 The commentary is quoting the verses so the quotation is placed in italics here, using italics in the same way as in the English translation above.
9 (P)33, (N)33 "bsdu bar". (P)17, (N)17, (D)17, (C)17 "bsdu ba".
10 (P)17, (N)17 "blta ba". (P)33, (N)33, (D)17, (C)17 "lta ba".
11 (P)17, (N)17, (D)17, (C)17 "de". (P)33, (N)33 "de la".
12 (P)17, (P)33, (N)17, (N)33 "gi". (D)17 and (C)17 omit it.
13 (P)17, (N)17, (N)33, (D)17, (C)17 "gyis". (P)33 "gyi".
14 (P)17, (N)17, (D)17, (C)17 " 'di skad ces bu". (P)33, (N)33 " 'di skad du".
15 (P)17, (N)17, (D)17, (C)17 "zhes". (P)33 and (N)33 omit it.
16 (P)33, (N)33 " 'di". (P)17, (N)17, (D)17, (C)17 " 'dis".
17 (P)17, (P)33, (N)17, (N)33 "rnams". (D)17, (C)17 "rnam".
18 (P)17, (N)17, (D)17, (C)17 "na". (P)33 and (N)33 omit it.
19 (P)17, (N)17, (D)17, (C)17 "yan lag tu gyur pa". (P)33, (N)33 " 'gyur bar" alone.
20 None of the relevant Dunhuang Manuscripts (Pelliot 114A, 762, 763, 764, 765, 766 and Stein 623, 621.2 and 622) include "dang thugs" or a reasonable equivalent here.
21 (P)17, (N)17, (D)17, (C)17 "na". (P)33 and (N)33 omit it.
22 The Sanskrit relationship between "muni" and forms of "mauna" does not translate particularly well, hence Tibetan "thub pa" and "thub pas" are found with no underlying implication of "silence".

gsungs pa[1] zhes bya ba ni bstan pa dang bshad pa[2] zhes[3] bya ba'i rnam[4] grangs su gtogs pa'o // de yang rang bzhin dang / nges pa dang / skyes bu dang /[5] gzhan la rag las pa dang / dbang phyug dang / dus dang / ngo bo nyid dang / 'dod rgyal dang / gnam gyis bskos pa[6] dang / gyi na la sogs pa'i[7] rgyu rnams[8] las byung ba[9] ni ma yin te[10] / 'di ni rten cing 'brel par 'byung ba'o // yan lag bye brag[11] bcu gnyis po 'di[12] dag ni nyon mongs pa dang / las dang / sdug bsngal rnams su[13] gcig la gcig brten te[14] mdung khyim gyi tshul du gsum po dag tu zad par 'dus par[15] 'gyur ro // zad par zhes bya ba ni ma lus par zhes bya ba'i tha tshig go /

dris pa / nyon mongs pa rnams ni gang / las dag[16] ni gang / sdug bsngal ni gang / rten pa'i bye brag 'di dag gang du ji ltar[17] bsdu bar 'gyur /

smras pa / *dang po brgyad dang dgu nyon mongs* // bye brag bcu gnyis kyi dang po ni ma rig pa / brgyad pa ni sred pa[18] / dgu pa ni len pa ste / 'di gsum[19] ni nyon mongs pa rnams su shes par bya'o //

las de gang zhe na / *gnyis dang bcu pa las yin te* / gnyis pa ni 'du byed / bcu pa ni srid pa[20] ste / chos 'di[21] gnyis ni las su bsdu bar[22] shes par bya'o //

lhag ma bdun yang sdug bsngal yin // nyon mongs pa dang / las su

1 (P)17, (N)17, (D)17, (C)17 "gsungs pa". (P)33, (N)33 "gsungs".
2 Sanskrit "kathita" and "prakaśita" (not "śāsana" and "ākhytātā").
3 (P)17, (N)17, (D)17, (C)17 "bshad pa zhes". (P)33, (N)33 "bshad ces".
4 (P)33, (N)33, (D)17, (C)17 "rnam". (P)17 and (N)17 omit it.
5 (P)17, (N)17, (D)17, (C)17 "dang /". (P)33 and (N)33 omit it.
6 (D)17, (C)17 "gnam gyis bskos pa". (P)17, (N)17 "gnas kyis bskos pa". (P)33, (N)33 "gnas kyis bskal pa".
7 (P)17, (N)17, (D)17, (C)17 "la sogs pa'i". (P)33, (N)33 "log pa'i".
8 (P)17, (N)17, (D)17, (C)17 "rnams". (P)33 and (N)33 omit it.
9 Sanskrit "aṇuprasūtāḥ" and not the expected "hetu-prasūtāḥ".
10 (P)17, (N)17, (D)17, (C)17 "te". (P)33, (N)33 "gyi".
11 (P)17, (N)17 "bye brag". (P)33, (N)33, (D)17 and (C)17 omit it.
12 (P)17, (N)17, (D)17, (C)17 " 'di". (P)33, (N)33 "de".
13 (P)17, (N)17, (D)17, (C)17 "su". (P)33 and (N)33 omit it.
14 (D)17, (C)17 "brten te". (P)17, (N)17 "rten te". (P)33, (N)33 "brten pa".
15 (P)17, (N)17, (D)17, (C)17 " 'dus par". (P)33 and (N)33 omit it.
16 (P)17, (N)17, (D)17, (C)17 "dag". (P)33 and (N)33 omit it.
17 (P)17, (N)17, (D)17, (C)17 "ji ltar". (P)33 and (N)33 omit it.
18 (P)33, (N)17, (N)33 "sred pa". (P)17 "sreg pa". (D)17, (C)17 "srid pa".
19 (P)17, (N)17, (D)17, (C)17 " 'di gsum". (P)33, (N)33 "gsum pa".
20 (P)17, (N)33, (D)17, (C)17 "srid pa". (P)33, (N)17 "sred pa".
21 (P)17, (N)17, (D)17, (C)17 " 'di". (P)33 and (N)33 omit it.
22 (P)17, (N)17, (D)17, (C)17 "bsdu bar". (P)33, (N)33 " 'dus par".

bsdus pa'i bye brag de dag gi lhag ma bye brag bdun po gang yin pa de dag ni[1] sdug bsngal du bsdu bar[2] shes par bya ste[3] / 'di lta ste / rnam par shes pa dang / ming dang gzugs dang / skye mched drug dang / reg pa dang / tshor ba dang / skye ba dang / rga shi rnams so // yang zhes bya ba'i sgra ni bsdu ba ste / sdug pa[4] dang bral ba dang / mi sdug pa dang phrad pa dang / 'dod pas phongs pa'i sdug bsngal rnams sdud pa'o[5] //

bcu gnyis chos ni gsum du 'dus //[6] de'i phyir chos bcu gnyis po de[7] dag ni las dang nyon mongs pa dang[8] sdug bsngal rnams su shes par bya'o // ni zhes bya ba'i sgra[9] ni lhag ma'i tshig[10] bcad pa'i don te[11] / mdo las bstan pa'i chos rnams[12] ni 'di dag tu zad kyi de[13] las gzhan ci yang med do zhes bcad pa'o //

dris pa / de dag[14] ni[15] 'tshal na nyon mongs pa dang las dang sdug bsngal 'di dag ni[16] gang las gang byung ba[17] bstan du gsol //

smras pa / *gsum po dag las*[18] *gnyis 'byung ste* // nyon mongs pa zhes bya ba[19] gsum po dag las / las zhes bya ba gnyis 'byung ngo // *gnyis las bdun 'byung* // sdug bsngal zhes bya ba gong du bstan pa rnams so // *bdun*

1 (P)33, (N)33, (D)17, (C)17 "ni". (P)17, (N)17 "gi".
2 (P)17, (N)17, (D)17, (C)17 "bsdu bar". (P)33 and (N)33 omit it.
3 (P)17, (N)17, (D)17, (C)17 "bya ste". (P)33, (N)33 "bya'o".
4 (P)17, (P)33, (N)33, (D)17, (C)17 "pa". (N)17 "par".
5 (P)17, (N)17, (D)17, (C)17 "sdud pa'o". (P)33, (N)33 "bsdu ste".
6 (P)33, (N)33, (D)17, (C)17 "*bcu gnyis chos ni gsum du 'dus //*". (P)17 and (N)17 omit this.
7 (P)17, (N)17, (D)17, (C)17 "de". (P)33, (N)33 " 'di".
8 (P)17, (P)33, (N)17, (D)17, (C)17 "dang". (N)33 "nas /".
9 (P)17, (N)17 "sgra". (P)33, (N)33, (D)17, (C)17 "sgras".
10 (P)17, (N)17 "lhag ma'i tshig". (D)17, (C)17 "lhag ma'i tshigs". (P)33, (N)33 "lhag pa'i tshigs".
11 (P)17, (N)17, (D)17, (C)17 "te". (P)33, (N)33 "to".
12 (P)17, (N)17, (D)17, (C)17 "rnams". (P)33 and (N)33 omit it.
13 (P)17, (N)17, (D)17, (C)17 "de". (P)33, (N)33 "/ 'di".
14 Sanskrit singular "etad".
15 (P)17, (N)17, (D)17, (C)17 "ni". (P)33 and (N)33 omit it.
16 (P)17, (N)17, (D)17, (C)17 " 'di dag ni". (P)33, (N)33 "dag".
17 (P)17, (N)17, (D)17 and (C)17 "byung ba". (P)33, (N)33 " 'byung ba de dag". Sanskrit "kutaḥ kiṃ udbhavati" in the Lhasa manuscript. Sanskrit "kutaḥ kiṃ saṃkramati" in the Gilgit manuscript might suggest "...what transfers and from where".
18 (P)33, (N)33, (D)17, (C)17 "*las*". (P)17, (N)17 "*la*".
19 (P)33, (N)33 "zhes bya ba". (P)17, (N)17, (D)17 and (C)17 omit it.

las kyang gsum 'byung // nyon mongs pa[1] zhes bya ba rnams so // yang nyon mongs pa zhes bya ba[2] gsum po de dag las / las[3] gnyis 'byung ste /[4] *srid pa'i 'khor lo de / nyiḍ ni yang dang yang du 'khor* // srid pa ni gsum ste / 'dod pa dang / gzugs dang / gzugs med pa zhes bya ste / de[5] dag tu mi sdod par[6] 'khor ba'i 'khor lor[7] gyur pa so so'i skye bo'i 'jig rten 'di nyid bdag nyid[8] kun tu 'phyan to[9] // ni[10] zhes bya ba'i sgra[11] ni nges pa med par bstan pa'i don te[12] // ji ltar 'khor lo rim gyis[13] 'khor ba de ltar srid pa rnams su 'byung ba yang ma yin gyi[14] nges pa med par bstan to //

dris pa / 'o na[15] lus thams cad kyi dbang phyug sems can zhes bgyi ba gang lags / de'i bgyid pa ji lta bu[16] /

smras pa / *'gro*[17] *kun*[18] *rgyu dang 'bras bu ste*[19] // btags pa[20] ma

1 (P)17, (P)33, (N)33, (N)17 "pa". (D)17 and (C)17 omit it.
2 (P)17, (N)17 have "zhes bya ba". (D)17, (C)17 have "rnams". (P)33 and (N)33 have neither.
3 (P)17, (N)17, (D)17, (C)17 "/ las". (P)33 and (N)33 omit it.
4 The Sanskrit is more concise here.
5 (P)17, (N)17, (D)17, (C)17 "gzugs med pa zhes bya ste / de". (P)33, (N)33 "gzugs med pa".
6 (P)17, (P)33, (N)17, (N)33 "mi sdod par". (D)17 "mi 'dod par". (C)17 "ni 'dod par".
7 (P)17, (P)33, (N)17, (N)33, (D)17 "lor". (C)17 "yor".
8 (P)17, (N)17, (D)17, (C)17 " 'di nyid bdag nyid". (P)33, (N)33 " 'di dag nyid".
9 (P)33, (N)33 "to". (D)17, (C)17 "no". (P)17 and (N)17 have neither.
10 Sanskrit "tu".
11 (P)17, (N)17, (D)17, (C)17 "sgra". (P)33, (N)33 "sgras".
12 (D)17, (C)17 "te". (P)17, (N)17 "ste". (P)33, (N)33 "to".
13 (P)17, (N)17, (D)17, (C)17 "rim gyis". (P)33, (N)33 "rin po che".
14 (P)17, (N)17, (D)17, (C)17 "srid pa rnams su 'byung ba yang ma yin gyi". (P)33, (N)33 "srid pa gsum du 'byung ba ma yin gyi /".
15 (P)33, (N)33, (D)17, (C)17 " 'o na". (P)17, (N)17 "kho na".
16 (D)17, (C)17 "bgyi ba gang lags / de'i bgyid pa ji lta bu". (P)17, (N)17 "bgyi ba gang lags / de'i bgyid pa ji ltar bur". (P)33, (N)33 "bgyi ba de dag las de byed pa ji lta bu".
17 (P)17 and (N)17 add "ba". (P)33, (N)33, (D)17 and (C)17 omit it.
18 (P)17 and (N)17 add "gyi". (P)33,(N)33, (D)17, and (C)17 omit it.
19 (P)17, (N)17, (D)17, (C)17 " *'bras bu ste*". (P)33, (N)33 "brtson 'grus te".
20 (P)17, (N)17, (D)17, (C)17 "btags pa". (P)33, (N)33 "brtag pa".

gtogs par / *'di la sems can gzhan ci'ang*[1] *med* // 'di ni[2] yang dag par brtags pa[3] ste / brtags pa tsam[4] ni ma yin no // brtags pa tsam du yod pa de[5] ni rdzas su yod par[6] mi rung ngo //

dris pa / gal te de ltar[7] na / 'o na 'jig rten 'di nas 'jig rten[8] pha rol tu su mchi[9] /

smras pa / 'di nas 'jig rten[10] pha rol tu rdul phra mo tsam yang mi 'pho ste / 'on kyang / *stong pa kho na'i chos rnams las* // *stong pa'i chos rnams 'byung bar zad* // bdag dang bdag gi med pa'i chos // nyon mongs pa dang las zhes bya ba rgyur gyur pa lnga po stong pa rnams las / bdag dang bdag gi med pa[11] sdug bsngal du brjod pa / 'bras bur brtag pa'i[12] chos stong pa bdun po de dag[13] 'byung bar 'gyur ro[14] zhes bya ba'i tha tshig go // de ni 'di skad du / bdag dang bdag gi med la /[15] de dag phan tshun du yang bdag dang bdag gi[16] ma yin te / 'on kyang rang bzhin gyis bdag med pa'i chos rnams las rang bzhin gyis[17] bdag med pa'i chos rnams 'byung ba de ltar khong du chud par bya'o // zhes[18] bstan pa yin no //

1 (P)33, (N)33 "*gzhan ci'ang*". (D)17, (C)17 "*ci yang*". (P)17, (N)17 "*gzhan ci yang*", against the metre.

2 In order to avoid the horror of documenting variants in different printings of the same edition — here (D)17 — we shall assume the "i" has worn off the Delhi printing's original blocks, explaining the reprint "na" while the Tokyo facsimile edition has a clear "ni".

3 (P)33, (N)33, (D)17, (C)17 "brtags pa". (P)17, (N)17 "btags pa".

4 (P)17, (N)17, (D)17, (C)17 add "gyi tshul du". (P)33 and (N)33 omit it.

5 (P)17, (N)17, (D)17, (C)17 "tsam du yod pa de". (P)33, (N)33 "tsam gyi yul du 'dod pa".

6 Suggesting Sanskrit "dravyasat", "substantial existence" as opposed to "prajñaptisat", "conceptual existence".

7 (P)17, (N)17, (D)17, (C)17 "ltar". (P)33, (N)33 "lta".

8 (P)17, (N)17, (D)17, (C)17 " 'jig rten". (P)33, (N)33 omit it.

9 (D)17, (C)17 "su mchi". (P)17, (N)17 "su la mchi". (P)33, (N)33 "su 'chi".

10 (P)17, (N)17, (D)17, (C)17 " 'di nas 'jig rten". (P)33, (N)33 " 'jig rten 'di nas".

11 (P)17, (N)17, (D)17, (C)17 "med pa". (P)33, (N)33 "med pa'i".

12 (P)33, (N)33 "brtag pa'i". (P)17, (N)17, (D)17, (C)17 "btags pa'i".

13 (P)17, (N)17 "de dag". (D)17, (C)17 "dag". (P)33 and (N)33 have neither.

14 (P)17, (N)17, (D)17, (C)17 "ro". (P)33 and (N)33 omit it.

15 (P)17, (N)17, (D)17, (C)17 "bdag gi med la /". (P)33, (N)33 "bdag med pa".

16 (P)17, (N)17, (D)17, (C)17 "yang bdag dang bdag gi". (P)33, (N)33 "yang dang yang bdag gi ba".

17 (D)17, (C)17 "gyis". (P)17, (P)33, (N)17, (N)33 "gyi".

18 (P)33, (N)17, (N)33, (D)17, (C)17 "zhes". (P)17, "zhas".

'dir dris pa /[1] rang bzhin gyis bdag med pa'i chos de kho na[2] dag las rang bzhin gyis[3] bdag med pa'i chos[4] 'byung ba 'di[5] la dpe ci mchis /

'dir smras pa[6] / *kha ton*[7] *mar me me long rgya*[8] // *me shel sa bon skyur dang sgras*[9] // dpe 'di rnams dang[10] brtags pas[11] kyang rang bzhin gyis bdag med pa dang 'jig rten pha rol 'grub par[12] shes par bya'o //

dper na bla ma'i kha nas brjod pa rnams slob ma la 'pho ba[13] ni bla mas brjod du[14] med par[15] 'gyur bas mi 'pho'o // slob mas smra ba[16] yang / gzhan las ma yin te / rgyu med par 'gyur ba'i phyir ro // ji ltar bla ma'i kha nas brjod pa ltar 'chi ka'i[17] sems kyang de bzhin te / rtag pa'i skyon du 'gyur bas / 'jig rten pha rol tu mi 'gro'o // 'jig rten pha rol yang gzhan las mi 'byung ste / rgyu med pa'i[18] skyon du 'gyur ba'i phyir ro // ji ltar bla mas brjod pa'i rgyu las 'byung bas[19] slob ma[20] de nyid dang de dag[21] gzhan no zhes brjod[22] par mi nus pa ltar 'chi ka'i[23] sems la brten nas

1 (P)17, (N)17 "dris pa /". (D)17, (C)17 "smras pa /". (P)33 and (N)33 have neither.

2 (P)33, (N)33 "de kho na". (P)17, (N)17, (D)17 and (C)17 omit it.

3 (P)33, (N)33, (D)17, (C)17 "gyis". (P)17, (N)17 "gyi".

4 (P)17, (N)17, (D)17 and (C)17 add "kho na dag". (P)33 and (N)33 omit it.

5 (P)17, (N)17, (D)17, (C)17 " 'di". (P)33, (N)33 "de".

6 (P)17, (N)17, (N)33, (D)17, (C)17 "smras pa". (P)33 "smas pa".

7 (P)17, (P)33 (N)17, (N)33, "*ton*". (D)17, (C)17 "th*on*".

8 (P)33, (N)33, (D)17, (C)17 "*rgya*". (P)17, (N)17 "b*rgya*".

9 (P)17, (N)17, (D)17, (C)17 "*sgras*". (P)33, (N)33 "*sgra*".

10 (P)17, (N)17, (D)17 and (C)17 "dang". (P)33 and (N)33 omit it.

11 (P)17, (P)33, (N)17, (N)33, "brtags pas". (D)17, (C)17 "bcas pas".

12 (P)33, (N)33, (D)17 and (C)17 " 'grub par". (P)17 and (N)17 omit it.

13 (P)17, (N)17, (D)17, (C)17 "slob ma la 'pho ba". (P)33, (N)33 "slob mar 'pho na".

14 (P)17, (N)17, (D)17, (C)17 "brjod du". (P)33, (N)33 "brjod pa de".

15 (P)33 and (N)33 add "yang". (P)17, (N)17, (D)17 and (C)17 omit it.

16 (P)17, (N)17, (D)17, (C)17 "smra ba". (P)33, (N)33 "smras pa".

17 (P)33, (N)33 " 'chi ka'i". (P)17, (N)17, (D)17, (C)17 " 'chi kha'i".

18 (P)17, (P)33, (N)33, (D)17, (C)17 "rgyu med pa'i". (N)17 certainly does not have "rgyu med pa'i", but what it does have is illegible. It looks something like "sgyud ma'i".

19 (D)17, (C)17 " 'byung bas". (P)17, (N)17 " 'byung ba". (P)33 and (N)33 omit it.

20 Sanskrit "śiṣyasyādhyayanaṃ" as well as "guroradhyayana" might suggest "slob mas smra ba" could have been expected here.

21 (P)17, (N)17, (D)17, (C)17 "de dag. (P)33 and (N)33 omit it. Here "de las" could have been expected.

22 (P)17 and (N)17 omit "brjod". (P)33, (N)33, (D)17 and (C)17 include it. Such an omission shows how close to each other the Peking and sNar thang editions can be, even where an error is unambiguously clear to any reader.

23 (P)33, (N)33 " 'chi ka'i". (P)17, (N)17, (D)17, (C)17 " 'chi kha'i".

skye ba'i char gtogs pa'i[1] sems kyang de bzhin te / de dag[2] nyid dang de las gzhan[3] zhes brjod par mi nus so //

de bzhin du ji ltar[4] mar me[5] las mar me dang / bzhin las me long gi gzugs brnyan 'byung ba dang / rgya las rgya'i 'bur dang / me shel las me dang /[6] sa bon las myu gu dang / shing tog skyur mo'i chu las[7] 'gram chu ldang ba dang / sgra las brag ca[8] 'byung bar 'gyur zhing / de dag kyang de nyid dang[9] gzhan no zhes[10] shes par sla ba[11] ma yin pa de bzhin du /

phung po nying mtshams sbyor ba yang // mi 'pho bar yang mkhas rtogs[12] *bya* // de la phung po[13] ni / gzugs dang / tshor ba dang / 'du shes dang / 'du byed dang / rnam par shes pa'i phung po'o // de dag gi[14] nying mtshams sbyor ba zhes bya ba[15] ni / 'gags nas rgyu de las 'bras bu[16] gzhan dag 'byung ba ste / 'jig rten 'di nas 'jig rten[17] pha rol tu dngos po rdul phra mo tsam yang mi 'gro'o / de ltar na 'khor ba'i 'khor lo ni[18] nor ba'i rnam par rtog pa'i bag chags kyis bskyed pa yin no // tha ma'i yang zhes pa'i sgra[19] ni ldog pa ste / de las bzlog par[20] shes par bya'o //

dngos po rnams la mi rtag pa dang / sdug bsngal ba dang / stong pa

1 (P)33, (N)33 "skye ba'i char rtogs pa'i". (D)17, (C)17 "skyes pa'i char gtogs pa'i". (P)17, (N)17 "skye bar gtogs pa'i".
2 (P)17, (N)17, (D)17, (C)17 "de dag". (P)33, (N)33 "bdag".
3 (P)33, (N)33 add "no". (P)17, (N)17, (D)17 and (C)17 omit it.
4 (P)17, (P)33, (N)17, (N)33 "ji ltar". (D)17 and (C)17 omit it.
5 (P)33, (N)33, (D)17, (C)17 "mar me". (P)17, (N)17 "me".
6 The Sanskrit is rather different for this one illustration: "ādityamaṇigomayaprasutyā vahni".
7 (P)33, (N)33 "shing tog skyur mo'i chu las". (P)17 "shing thog skyur po'i skyus". (N)17, (D)17, (C)17 "shing thog skyur po'i rgyus".
8 (P)17, (N)17, (D)17, (C)17 "brag ca". (P)33, (N)33 "brag cha".
9 (P)33, (N)33 add "de las". (P)17, (N)17, (D)17 and (C)17 omit it.
10 (P)33, (N)33 "no zhes". (P)17, (N)17, (D)17 and (C)17 omit it.
11 (P)17, (N)17, (N)33, (D)17, (C)17 "sla ba". (P)33 "slo ba".
12 (P)17, (P)33, (N)17, (N)33 "*rtogs*". (D)17, (C)17 "*rtog*".
13 (P)33, (N)33 add "lnga" here. (P)17, (N)17, (D)17 and (C)17 omit it.
14 (P)33, (N)33 "gi". (P)17, (N)17, (D)17 and (C)17 omit it.
15 (P)17, (N)17, (D)17, (C)17 "zhes bya ba". (P)33 and (N)33 omit it.
16 (P)33, (N)33 " 'bras bu". (P)17, (N)17, (D)17, (C)17 " 'byung ba".
17 (P)33 and (N)33 include this " 'jig rten". (P)17, (N)17, (D)17 and (C)17 omit it.
18 (P)33, (N)33 " 'khor lo ni". (P)17, (N)17, (D)17, (C)17 " 'khor lor".
19 (P)17, (N)17, (D)17, (C)17 "zhes pa'i sgra". (P)33, (N)33 "zhes bya ba".
20 (P)17, (N)17, (D)17, (C)17 "bzlog par". (P)33, (N)33 "zlog par".

dang / bdag med par rtogs[1] na / dngos po[2] la rmongs par mi 'gyur ro // rmongs pa med na mi chags so // ma chags na zhe sdang bar mi 'gyur ro // zhe sdang[3] med na las mi byed do // las med na dngos po mi len no // len pa med na srid pa mngon par 'du mi byed do // srid pa med na mi skye'o // ma skyes na lus dang sems[4] la sdug bsngal mi 'byung ngo // de ltar 'dir rgyu lnga po de[5] ma bsags pas gzhan du 'bras bu[6] mi 'byung ste / 'di ni thar pa zhes bya'o // de ltar na rtag pa dang chad pa'i mtha'[7] la sogs pa lta ba ngan pa rnams bsal ba[8] yin no //

'di la tshigs su bcad pa gnyis yod de /

shin tu phra ba'i dngos la yang //
gang gis[9] chad par rnam brtags pa[10] //
rnam par mi mkhas de yis[11] ni //
rkyen las 'byung ba'i[12] don ma mthong //

'di la bsal bya[13] gang yang med //
gzhag par[14] bya ba ci yang med //
yang dag nyid la yang dag blta[15] //
yang dag mthong na[16] rnam par grol //

rten cing 'brel par 'byung ba'i snying po'i rnam par bshad pa / slob

1 (P)17, (N)17, (D)17, (C)17 "rtogs". (P)33 "brtag". (N)33 "rtag".
2 (P)33, (N)33 add "rnams". (P)17, (N)17, (D)17 and (C)17 omit it.
3 (P)17, (N)17, (D)17, (C)17 "zhe sdang". (P)33, (N)33 "zhe sdang ba".
4 In the Dunhuang manuscripts "sems" is found alone, without "lus dang". (See footnote 26 on p. 109 below.)
5 (P)17, (N)17, (D)17, (C)17 add "dag". (P)33 and (N)33 omit it.
6 (P)17, (N)17, (D)17, (C)17 "gzhan du 'bras bu". (P)33, (N)33 " 'bras bu gzhan du".
7 (P)17, (N)17, (D)17, (C)17 "rtag pa dang chad pa'i mtha'". (P)33, (N)33 "rtag chad".
8 (P)17, (P)33, (N)17, (N)33 "bsal ba". (D)17, (C)17 "gsal ba".
9 (P)17, (P)33, (N)17, (N)33 "*gis*". (D)17, (C)17 "*gi*".
10 (P)17, (N)17 "*brtags pa*". (P)33, (N)33 "*brtag pa*". (D)17, (C)17 "*brtags par*".
11 (P)17, (P)33, (N)17, (N)33 "*yis*". (D)17, (C)17 "*yi*".
12 (P)33, (N)33 " *'byung ba'i*". (P)17, (N)17, (D)17, (C)17 "skyes pa'i".
13 (P)17, (N)17, (N)33 "*bsal bya*". (P)33 "bsal ba". (D)17, (C)17 "*gsal bya*".
14 (P)33, (N)33, (D)17, (C)17 "*gzhag par*". (P)17, (N)17 "b*zhag par*".
15 (P)17, (N)17, (D)17, (C)17 "*blta*". (P)33, (N)33 "*lta*".
16 (D)17, (C)17 "*na*" (P)17, (P)33, (N)17, (N)33 "*nas*".

dpon[1] klu sgrub kyis mdzad pa rdzogs so // //[2] rgya gar gyi mkhan po dzi na mi tra dang / dha na shi la dang / shi le' ndra bo dhe[3] dang / ba nde ye shes sdes la sogs pas bsgyur cing zhus te gtan la phab bo[4] //

1 (P)33 and (N)33 add " 'phags pa". (P)17, (N)17, (D)17 and (C)17 omit it.

2 (P)33, (N)33, (D)17 and (C)17 omit the following information. (P)17 and (N)17 include it. Hakuju Ui's A complete catalogue of the Tibetan Buddhist Canons (bkaḥ-ḥgyur and bstan-ḥgyur) (the Tōhoku catalogue, No. 3837, p. 579) gives the translators of the Pratītyasamutpādahṛdayavyākhyāna as Ānanda and Grags 'byor shes rab. They were one of the translating teams for the Mahāyānaviṃśikā but there does not seem to be any evidence for taking them to be translators of the Pratītyasamutpādahṛdayavyākhyāna. Certainly the sDe dge text to which the catalogue entry refers does not mention them.

3 In fact both (P)17 and (N)17 look more like "bhe" than "dhe".

4 (P)17 "phab bo". (N)17 "phab ba'". The orthography of these texts in the sNar thang edition almost lets this variation go unremarked. As is often the case, where appropriate "ba" is read for what can be a quite clear "pa" in the Tibetan printing. More relevant here is the lack of a "na ro", but this may have no significance as these sNar thang texts often leave out or distort obvious vowels above the line, and it would be far too cumbersome to note each instance. The " 'a chung" is more noteworthy.

Comments

The three texts translated and edited in this work are based upon Tibetan translations in the light of their extant Sanskrit versions. The detail below sets the scene for an understanding of the sources.

For each of the three texts we have two Tibetan translations in the Tibetan canon. For each of the three texts we have Sanskrit manuscripts, one complete one for the Mahāyānaviṃśikā, two for the Pratītyasamutpāda-hṛdayakārikā with its commentary incomplete in each. For the Mahāyāna-viṃśikā we also have Tibetan quotations in other texts of some of its verses. For the Pratītyasamutpādahṛdayakārikā we have Sanskrit and Tibetan quotations in other texts of some of its verses. For the Pratītyasamutpāda-hṛdayakārikā we also have earlier Dunhuang manuscripts of the Pratītya-samutpādahṛdayakārikā, of its commentary and of a commentary on the commentary. The translators have come up with different results; sometimes the variations are considerable — especially with the Mahāyāna-viṃśikā — sometimes the translations are almost identical. Their Sanskrit sources will also have been identical in some instances, varying in others.

Almost limitless comparison and speculation can be made in comparing the Tibetan translations, but one example will serve to show how far two teams of translators can seem to vary from each other. The Mahāyānaviṃśikā provides the better examples for wild variations. One of the less puzzling ones is the verse asking about not embarking on the Great Vehicle. Candrakumāra and Sha' kya 'od's translation of that particular verse is a model of clarity[1] while Ānanda and Grags 'byor shes rab's translation of the verse is a model of confusion,[2] yet the weaker translation even with its missing line is not emended in the light of the other translation. This lack of influence of one translation of the Mahāyānaviṃśikā on the other makes the comparison of the two valuable for some insight into the ways of Tibetan translation from Sanskrit. It

1 See p. 46 above, (verse 22). Their translation is precise enough to follow the divisions and the order of the Sanskrit pādas, while retaining good style and expressing the ideas clearly.

2 It is confused in the form in which it has come down to us, though the original translation may well have been sound, see p. 37 above, (verse 20).

would appear that no consolidation of the two translations in the light of each other has taken place. The considerable variation between the two is the probable reason that both have been preserved in the Tibetan tradition, rather than one superseding, or even simply influencing, the other.

The same verse is also available as a quotation in Dharmendra's Tattvasārasaṃgraha. When all three versions are compared it is clear that no one version is a copy of another, all can give insight into the independent translating of the verse from the Sanskrit.

In the edited Tibetan above, and in the comments below, many more variations are considered, particularly in the Mahāyānaviṃśikā, but also in the Pratītyasamutpādahṛdayakārikā and Pratītyasamutpādahṛdaya-vyākhyāna. The balancing of all these considerations is the means by which a reader can try to see just what Nāgārjuna had in mind. While the edited texts should be rigidly faithful to the textual evidence, the English translations are much more interpretive, attempting to mirror for the English language the Tibetan principle for translators and revisors: "The style for translating the sacred teachings is to use good Tibetan while not violating the sense".[1]

1 This often quoted statement is found in the sGra sbyor, followed by a sentence with a less subjective tone: "When translating the teachings do not disturb the Sanskrit word order, translate into Tibetan adhering to the sense and to the words, translate well and correctly." ("dam pa'i chos bsgyur ba'i lugs ni don dang yang mi 'gal la bod skad la yang gar bde bar gyis shig / dharmma bsgyur ba la rgya gar gyi skad kyi go rims las mi bsnor bar bod kyi skad du bsgyur na don dang tshig tu 'brel zhing bde na ma nor bar sgyur cig /") (Peking bstan 'gyur — mdo 'grel 124 (ngo) 2b6–2b7). The second sentence in the quotation is a bit more demanding than the first and while its suggestions may be impossible when translating into English it was hardly rigidly adhered to in matters of Sanskrit word order even in the most wooden Tibetan translations. A balance between incompatible aims was presumably intended, and all such methods are bound to fall short of ideals.

The Mahāyānaviṃśikā

In part one it was pointed out that the Mahāyānaviṃśikā is attributed to Nāgārjuna in its Chinese and Tibetan versions, as well as elsewhere in Tibetan tradition.[1]

It was also mentioned there that the Mahāyānaviṃśikā translated in this work is largely that of the Tibetan tradition, a version translated into Tibetan by the Kashmiri paṇḍit Ānanda and the Tibetan translator Grags 'byor shes rab.[2] Here in part two the edited Tibetan of that version appears first, followed for comparative purposes by a version translated into Tibetan by the Indian paṇḍit Candrakumāra and the Tibetan translator Sha' kya 'od.[3]

Differences between versions of the Mahāyānaviṃśikā available to us were commented upon in general terms in the introduction to part one.[4] Details concerned with the significance of these differences are to be found in the edited Tibetan and throughout the comments on the study of the text below. It has also been made clear that the translation in part one is to some extent an attempt to put into readable English the content of Nagārjuna's text as it might have been at a stage much earlier than any of the surviving manuscripts. It may be unrealistic to aim to recreate for the reader of a translation the same effect that the original work would have had on its readers, yet such an aspiration does not seem a pointless ideal. Anyone

1 See p. 3.

2 Both Yamaguchi (his p. 176) and Bhattacharya (his p. 44) give Grags 'byor shes rab's name in Sanskrit: Kīrtibhūtiprajñā. Yamaguchi's "of Lotsāba" is the sort of embarrassing error best not dwelt upon.

Grags 'byor shes rab can be placed in the eleventh century and is known to have travelled to Kashmir. If this Ānanda is the well known Kashmiri translator Jayānanda he can also be placed in the eleventh century. (See: Naudou, Jean; Les bouddhistes kaśmīriens au Moyen Age, Paris : Presses universitaires de France, 1968, p. 171–174.)

3 Both Yamaguchi (his p. 176) and Bhattacharya (his p. 44) give Sha' kya 'od's name in Sanskrit: Śākyaprabhā. (Assuming Yamaguchi's "Śakhayaprabhā" is some sort of misprint.)

Sha' kya 'od can be placed in the eleventh century if it is accepted that he was a contemporary of Jñānaśrī, a Kashmiri translator of that time. (See: Naudou, Jean; op. cit., p. 177–181.) Together they translated the Guhyakoṣanāmamantraśastra (Peking 4688).

4 See p. 3.

doubting the validity of such speculative exercises is free to confine themselves to the surviving Sanskrit version of the text, perhaps viewing it in the light of Tibetan and Chinese translations.

The details about the available sources for the Mahāyānaviṃśikā are quite accessible and any serious reader of the text will wish to make use of at least three. The Sanskrit text from Ngor in Tibet was edited and translated by Giuseppe Tucci.[1] Vidhuśekhara Bhattacharya provided a reconstruction of the Sanskrit along with his edition of the Tibetan and Chinese versions many years before,[2] and he acknowledges the help of Tucci at that time with the Chinese. Susumu Yamaguchi also provides the Chinese and Tibetan texts, along with a translation; indeed his article was the inspiration for Bhattacharya's reconstruction of the Sanskrit.[3] Working through the details of these sources is a complicated task, but it is amply rewarding to have so much textual scholarship available.

Later quotations of the Mahāyānaviṃśikā provide alternative Tibetan translations from Sanskrit for some of the verses. Dharmendra's Tattvasāra-saṃgraha quotes verses 8/10, 9/11, 10/12, 20/22, /8, /9, and /18.[4] The quotations are given in footnotes to the appropriate verses in Candrakumāra and Sha' kya 'od's translation of the Mahāyānaviṃśikā. Āryadeva's Caryāmelāyanapradīpa quotes verse 18/19. That quotation is given in a footnote to the appropriate verse in Ānanda and Grags 'byor shes rab's translation of the Mahāyānaviṃśikā.

The striking thing about these quotations is that they are well done, in good Tibetan, but they are quite different to either Ānanda and Grags 'byor shes rab's or Candrakumāra and Sha' kya 'od's translations. Dharmendra's Tattvasārasaṃgraha was translated by Janārdana and Rin chen bzang po. Āryadeva's Caryāmelāyanapradīpa was translated by Śraddhākaravarman and Rin chen bzang po. The translations will have been made from the Sanskrit and there is no reason to suppose any Tibetan translations of the

1 Tucci, Giuseppe; Mahāyāna-viṃśikā of Nāgārjuna, p. 195–207, (section II of part I) in his Minor Buddhist texts, Roma, 1956.

2 Bhattacharya, Vidhuśekhara; Mahāyānaviṃśaka of Nāgārjuna, Calcutta, 1931 — (a reprint of his article in *The Visva-Bharati Quarterly*, Calcutta : 1930; 8: 107–150.)

3 Yamaguchi, Susumu; Nāgārjuna's Mahāyānaviṃśaka, *The Eastern Buddhist*, Kyoto, 1926; 4: 56–72, 1927; 4: 167–176.

4 The verse numbers here refer to the number in Ānanda and Grags 'byor shes rab's translation of the Mahāyānaviṃśikā, followed by an oblique stroke, followed by the number in Candrakumāra and Sha' kya 'od's translation of the Mahāyānaviṃśikā. Not all verses are in both sources.

Mahāyānaviṃśikā itself would have been consulted. To have another view for eight of the verses is helpful and perhaps more notable when one of the translators is the famous Rin chen bzang po.

So, for example, in the verse where the burning in hell is like bamboo on fire our main sources consist of only a Tibetan translation by Candrakumāra and Sha' kya 'od which has one line missing and the complete verse in the Sanskrit Ngor manuscript. Dharmendra's quotation strengthens the choice of "bamboo"[1] for what is burning and gives the Tibetan for all the lines of the verse.[2]

Tucci, in his Minor Buddhist Texts, provides further details about the paṇḍit Ānanda and the translator Sha' kya 'od,[3] as well as the expected introductory material on his Sanskrit manuscript.

The Sanskrit text from Ngor is surprising first and foremost because the expected first verse, the verse of invocation, appears as the eighth verse. The preceding verses seem to be an added introduction owing much to the Laṅkāvatāra.[4] The relationship of the remaining twenty-one verses with the other sources is clearly set out in Tucci's revision — in the light of the Sanskrit manuscript — of Bhattacharya's table of the order of verses in the various versions.[5] The variation is unimportant, but noticeable.

However, concentrating on differences it is easy to lose sight of the important fact that some seventeen of the verses do not vary inexplicably from our Tibetan text as translated by Ānanda and Grags 'byor shes rab.

Tucci decided it was useless for him to re-edit the Chinese and Tibetan translations,[6] but looking at either Yamaguchi or Bhattacharya's editions would suggest otherwise in the case of the Tibetan at least. Any of the Tibetan versions in the Tibetan canon in its unedited state is more reliable than either Yamaguchi or Bhattacharya's editions. Both Yamaguchi and Bhattacharya compound confusions which dissolve in the light of the Sanskrit, but Tucci leaves the reader to sort out such matters rather than giving any guidance. To give just one brief example by way of illustration, where Yamaguchi and Bhattacharya each reject "dogs pa",[7] and provide

1 Tibetan " 'od ma", Sanskrit "veṇu".
2 p. 41 above, (verse 8).
3 Tucci, Giuseppe; op. cit., p. 195.
4 See: ibid., p. 196 f.
5 Ibid. p. 198.
6 Tucci, Giuseppe; op. cit., p. 200.
7 Cf. p. 33 above.

their alternative possibilities, the Sanskrit "śankā" removes once and for all the need to emend against the textual evidence, or more precisely shows that there was no such need. More comment in general by Tucci on the significance of his Sanskrit readings would have been helpful in many instances.

Bhattacharya's work, particularly his reconstruction of the Sanskrit, is quite remarkable in itself but is of added interest in that it can now be compared with the subsequent availability of an authentic Sanskrit manuscript. The metre of the Sanskrit manuscript from Ngor is anuṣṭubh, which is the metre followed — on the whole quite strictly — in Bhattacharya's earlier reconstruction. In view of the difficulty of such an endeavour his achievement stands up well against the manuscript which inevitably supersedes it.[1] Not only does he provide a reconstructed Sanskrit version of the text, he has also translated individually each line of each verse in the two Tibetan versions and the Chinese version, the resulting Sanskrit translations being set out in his *Notes*.

Bhattacharya's Tibetan sources are confined to his own use of the sNar thang edition of the bstan 'gyur and what Yamaguchi reported of the Peking edition. Therefore his references to the Peking edition carry over any errors made by Yamaguchi; in fact wherever Bhattacharya refers to "P" it is safest to take him to mean "Yamaguchi".[2] He can favour a Yamaguchi erroneous reading against his own sNar thang text,[3] or reject one.[4] At times he is led into convoluted solutions to problems which do not really exist[5] but stem solely from accepting Yamaguchi's readings as an accurate indication of the Peking text. Anyone reading Bhattacharya in conjunction with a copy of the Peking edition of the text and nothing else would become hopelessly confused.

It would also be wise not to be too harsh in judging Bhattacharya's use of the sNar thang edition of his Tibetan text as it is an edition often poorly printed on very rough paper. Frequently letters are illegible to such an extent that any editor must make educated guesses in order to avoid being

1 N. Aiyaswami Sastri compiled a bibliography with a specific section for the interesting phenomenon of restored Sanskrit texts, see his: Ārya Śālistamba Sūtra, Madras, 1950, Appendix, p. xxxii-xxxiv.

2 E.g. his p. 18 n. 2, p. 19 n. 1 and n. 5, provide examples where Bhattacharya's references to "P" have nothing at all to do with the Peking edition of the text.

3 See his verse 17 n. 6 (p. 19). Cf. footnote to verse 10 (p. 33) above.

4 See his verse 18 n. 1 (p. 20). Cf. footnote to verse 10 (p. 33) above. Or see his verse 12 n. 1 (p. 19). Cf. footnote to verse 14 (p. 34) above.

5 See his *Notes* verse 6 (p. 31). Cf. footnote to verse 6 (p. 31) above.

submerged in trivial variants of obvious spellings, a procedure which is a clear invitation to minor errors.

In his *Notes* Bhattacharya also provides a number of references to and quotations from various relevant Buddhist texts, and this is a useful and valuable part of his work. His reference[1] to the comparison of his kārikā 22, asking about not embarking on the Great Vehicle, with Indrabhūti's Jñānasiddhi *XI* 8, should be a reference to SS 4 and the title is misspelt, but the comparison is worth making.[2] Though the Sanskrit of the Ngor manuscript is not identical with Indrabhūti's, the similarity is still very striking indeed. Bhattacharya concludes that Indrabhūti borrowed the verse from the Mahāyānaviṃśikā. On the other hand, this is the verse which Tucci thinks was a later addition to the original Mahāyānaviṃśikā — though it is found in the Sanskrit, in both Tibetan translations and in the Chinese translation. If its removal is accepted, along with the elimination of his first seven verses, this solution provides Tucci with the twenty verses required by a text entitled the Mahāyānaviṃśikā.[3] With regard to Bhattacharya's assertion on the source used by Indrabhūti, it seems to rest only on the fact that Indrabhūti makes deliberate quotations from other works. Bhattacharya makes a strong case for Indrabhūti having borrowed the verse, whereas his having borrowed the verse *specifically from the Mahāyānaviṃśikā* rests only on the fact that the verse can in fact be found there. However, the possibility of another source for both occurrences would suit both theories. Tucci then has a Sanskrit manuscript with what, on the surface at least, appears to be a core of twenty verses, with later additions attached.

In spite of the reconstruction of the Sanskrit text being superseded by a subsequent authentic Sanskrit manuscript and certain other reservations mentioned above, it should be said that careful use of Bhattacharya's work continues to provide much of interest to anyone delving deeply into the Mahāyānaviṃśikā.

Turning further back in time to Yamaguchi's treatment of the text, it is found to be a piece of work exceedingly well set out for comparison of the two Tibetan translations and the Chinese translation. He adheres to the order of Candrakumāra and Sha' kya 'od's translation, following each verse with

1 His p. 43; the reference is to p. 5.

2 For Indrabhūti's Jñānasiddhi *XI* 8, see: Bhattacharyya, Benoytosh; Two Vajrayāna Works, Baroda, 1929, p. 68.

3 Tucci, Giuseppe; op. cit. p. 199.

its equivalent in Ānanda and Grags 'byor shes rab's translation, and then its equivalent in Shih hu's Chinese translation. A year later his English translation with notes completed his work on the text.

His translation is based largely on Candrakumāra and Sha' kya 'od's Tibetan translation, rather than the Ānanda and Grags 'byor shes rab translation. The edition he uses is "the Red Peking" brought to Japan by Professor Yenga Teramoto.[1] This should correspond to my Peking edition, (P), but does not always do so.

Yamaguchi's *Notes* are quite fascinating, often suggesting Sanskrit readings not far from what was to come to light in the Ngor manuscript. Each instance is complicated given the various sources, but the results of considering his ideas can lead to an understanding of the text with fewer unresolved questions remaining, particularly in view of the Sanskrit now available.

For example, Yamaguchi suggests "śaraṇa"[2], corresponding to the Tibetan translation of Ānanda and Grags 'byor shes rab and the Chinese translation of Shih hu. But Candrakumāra and Sha' kya 'od's Tibetan translation has "snying po"[3] not "skyabs"[4], suggesting "sāra" not "śaraṇa" — Yamaguchi's "heart" not "shelter". Though the weight of evidence is on the side of Ānanda and Grags 'byor shes rab's translation Yamaguchi did not favour it in his translation. However, the added evidence of the Sanskrit does favour it; we find "śaraṇān" in the Ngor manuscript. This is often the pattern, Ānanda and Grags 'byor shes rab's translation providing the version more faithful to a Sanskrit source at first glance (rather than Candrakumāra and Sha' kya 'od's looser translation which Yamaguchi favours for his own translation) and then further confirmation of such a bias is found in the Sanskrit manuscript from Ngor.

From a Tibetan point of view the opposite translation might be favoured. Candrakumāra and Sha' kya 'od's translation provides the more sensible and easily readable translation rather than Ānanda and Grags 'byor shes rab's often puzzling and difficult to understand translation. If the aim is to provide a Tibetan translation to stand in isolation from a Sanskrit original Candrakumāra and Sha' kya 'od's work is undeniably preferable. But to attempt to imagine the Sanskrit placed before the Tibetan translators,

1 Yamaguchi, Susumu; op. cit., p. 59.
2 Ibid., p. 174.
3 p. 43 above, (verse 13).
4 p. 33 above, (verse 11).

Ānanda and Grags 'byor shes rab's work is the richer source. Could it be that their translation was originally meant to be read alongside the Sanskrit source? Certainly they translate the text pāda by pāda[1] paying scant attention to the requirements of ordinary Tibetan syntax.[2]

Yamaguchi is unhappy with Ānanda and Grags 'byor shes ṛab's Tibetan "nyam nga"[3] and how it fits in with Candrakumāra and Sha' kya 'od's Tibetan.[4] He suggests it stems from Sanskrit "saṃśaya"[5], "apprehension". However, we have accepted the Tibetan "dogs pa", "apprehension", which Yamaguchi had emended to "rtog pa". This "dogs pa" represents what is a straightforward synonym of "saṃśaya", Sanskrit "śaṇkā" found in the Ngor manuscript, and this meets Yamaguchi's requirements in the light of the

1 Or, verse by verse, in the sense of following the precise structure of the Sanskrit verse.

2 For an interesting detailed examination of translation from Sanskrit into Tibetan see Nils Simonsson's Indo-tibetische Studien : die Methoden der tibetischen Übersetzer, untersucht im Hinblick auf die Bedeutung ihrer Übersetzungen für die Sanskritphilologie, Uppsala, 1957. He compares and contrasts eighty-four verses and two short prose sections of the Saddharmapuṇḍarīka in Sanskrit and in three varying Tibetan translations. His Tibetan manuscript from Khotan displays a notably primitive translation technique, where usually each word in a pāda of the Sanskrit is represented in the corresponding Tibetan verse. This makes for very odd Tibetan, especially in matters like word order. In translating compound sentences covering two verses in the Sanskrit the grammatical correlation of the two verses can be omitted in the Tibetan. Simonsson also examines revised versions of his Tibetan translation, one canonical and one from Dunhuang. The revised versions pay much more attention to Tibetan syntax. The aim of the translators and revisors is not a translation of one Sanskrit manuscript deemed to be the best but an amalgam of various sources and influences, reflecting the readings of various manuscripts, weighing all these factors and yet producing one translation. Simonsson looks also at the Suvarṇaprabhāsa and he examines the Great Revision of the ninth century. Looking at translations of a late date he shows that verse by verse translation is no proof of a pre-Great Revision translation. He also presents selections from the Sgra sbyor or Madhyavyutpatti covering principles of translation.

See also Alfonsa Ferrari's Arthaviniścaya. Roma : 1944; 4: [535]-625.

For an analysis of Tibetan translating techniques in the sphere of medical literature see Claus Vogel's Vāgbhaṭa's Aṣṭāṅgahṛdayasaṃhitā, the first five chapters of its Tibetan version, accompanied by a literary introduction and a running commentary on the Tibetan translating-technique, Wiesbaden, 1965.

3 p. 33 above, (verse 10).

4 p. 43 above, (verse 12).

5 Yamaguchi, Susumu; op. cit., p. 174. Here misprints are not confined to the Tibetan — "ñam-na" for "ñam-ṅa" — but include "drived" for "derived".

Chinese also. However, that leaves "nyam nga", "anxieties", unaccounted for. It would seem to represent a reading of Sanskrit "viṣamā", rejecting Tucci's "viṣayā", "objects of experience". Tucci's reading was probably influenced by Candrakumāra and Sha' kya 'od's Tibetan "yul", but the rest of their line seems not to match the Sanskrit. If "viṣamā" is accepted — and many will consider such acceptance far too speculative — then Ānanda and Grags 'byor shes rab's translation seems to match the Sanskrit rather neatly. The clues and questions Yamaguchi provided can lead to answers because some of the further evidence he felt was needed is now available.

Yamaguchi poses other good questions. For example he asks of verse 3 "how can we reconcile this with *bshin-skhyes-pa-yi...*"[1] His "this" is the reading of Candrakumāra and Sha' kya 'od's translation and the Chinese translation. But the very Tibetan he quotes from Ānanda and Grags 'byor shes rab's translation provides a clue to a correction to Tucci's edition of the Ngor manuscript. Yamaguchi suggested a Sanskrit reading of "yoniśa utpannaḥ". For "skyes pa yi" he is essentially correct with "utpannaḥ", but "yoniśa" must be rejected, once the Sanskrit text is available. In considering Tucci's reading — "na cotpannāḥ" — support is found in Candrakumāra and Sha' kya 'od's Tibetan translation with "skye med pa". But what of Ānanda and Grags 'byor shes rab's "bzhin skyes pa yi"? Could it suggest a reading of "ivotpannāḥ", "iva" for "bzhin"? Then the line in Sanskrit would read "pārāvāram ivotpannāḥ". It fits rather nicely. And in fact this is one of the readings suggested by Lindtner in his footnote on Tucci's edition.

Indeed Lindtner has provided a very helpful footnote on Tucci's edition of the Ngor manuscript, suggesting much more than this one emendation. He gives considerably more weight to the Tibetan and Chinese texts than Tucci was willing to do.[2] For example he reads "adhīna" for Tucci's "dhīra" when the Tibetan has "dbang gyur".[3]

His most interesting point concerns the apparent loss of text in the Sanskrit manuscript from Ngor, his detection of "haplography".[4] Tucci's verse 6 is not what it might seem to be but is in fact the first three-quarters of one verse plus the second quarter of the next verse. In other words the

1 Ibid. p. 172. Misprinting "*skhyes*" for "*skyes*", his "sh" equals our "zh". See footnote to verse 3 (p. 30) above.

2 Lindtner, Christian; op. cit., p. 12 n. 16.

3 p. 33 above, (verse 11).

4 Lindtner, Christian; op. cit., p. 12 n. 16.

Sanskrit must once have had two verses of four pādas[1] each: 6 a, b, c, d and 7 a, b, c, d. But in the Ngor manuscript we find 6 a, b, c, 7 b posing as one verse. In the Tibetan, as it is set out, we can see each as a line, in the Sanskrit each is a half line. Originally both Sanskrit 6 c and 7 a must have each ended with the same word: "duḥkhaṃ".[2] At some point in making a copy of the text a jump from one "duḥkhaṃ" to the next happened and text went missing. Then 7 c and d would no longer fit the pattern of the poetry and would be tidied away, having taken on the appearance of an ill-fitting insertion. This applies only to the Ngor manuscript among our sources. Clearly the Sanskrit from which our Tibetan and Chinese translations stem had not suffered this textual error. This then explains the occurrence here of an apparent *extra* verse in both of the Tibetan translations and in the Chinese translation. It also seriously dents Tucci's theory about having uncovered the twenty verses of the text in the Ngor manuscript once later additions are taken into account.[3] Tucci's decision that the first seven verses in the Ngor Sanskrit manuscript are later additions is indisputable, but, if Lindtner's detection of haplography is accepted, Tucci's theory then requires the jettisoning of two further verses, not just the verse glorifying the Great Vehicle, in order to reach the required twenty verses which supported his hypothesis. This sort of evidence strengthens the value of the Tibetan and Chinese translations, even though we are dealing with what is originally a Sanskrit text.

Nevertheless could the Ngor Sanskrit manuscript be the weaker source by weight of numbers but the the less corrupt source to have come down to us? The single verse in the Ngor Sanskrit does make sense, it is perfectly readable. Nevertheless the weight of evidence seems to favour haplography as the explanation, the Sanskrit of the Ngor verse does not quite ring true and an alternative theory that all Chinese and Tibetan sources reflect a Sanskrit source with an expanded version of one verse is not very persuasive.

My own translation must favour the Tibetan, and on various occasions it provides alternatives preferable to the Sanskrit reading. One example mentioned in passing above[4] will suffice to illustrate the principle, — the apparent misreading of "viṣaya" ("object") for "viṣama" ("anxiety"). Tucci reads "viṣayā" in his verse 18 [11], though our text has Tibetan

1 "Quarter verses".
2 In our Tibetan translations "sdug bsngal".
3 Cf. p. 69 above.
4 p. 72.

"nyam nga", presumably reading Sanskrit "viṣamā".[1] While our text suggests this, the sense of the phrase reinforces the suggestion: "Their mistaken anxieties trouble them with the poison of apprehension."[2] Tucci's "objects of experience" fits the phrase less comfortably.[3]

On the other hand our favoured Tibetan text can suggest weak variants. In the verse where the artist frightens himself with his own creation the image in Ānanda and Grags 'byor shes rab's translation is of Yama, the god of the dead. However, the weight of evidence does not favour their Tibetan, though it is clear Ānanda and Grags 'byor shes rab read "yama" ("gshin rje").[4] In the other Tibetan translation Candrakumāra and Sha' kya 'od read "yakṣa" ("gnod sbyin").[5] In the Sanskrit manuscript from Ngor "yakṣa"[6] is found. The Chinese suggests "yakṣa". The simile itself is found elsewhere with a "yakṣa" ("goblin") as the artist's creation.[7] Clearly "yama" is unlikely to be the word used by Nāgārjuna. Though judgements are not made by simply adding up the occurrences of each possibility because an early error or variation can act as a source for many subsequent occurrences, the weight of evidence here clearly favours "yakṣa". The above two examples serve to give a flavour of the kind of detail which must be resolved in order to produce a plausible translation or an edited text.

Of those verses which appear in all sources — Sanskrit, Chinese and Tibetan — other than our own translation by Ānanda and Grags 'byor shes rab, all seem in varying degrees superfluous. For example:

1 See p. 33 above, (verse 10).

2 p. 33 above.

3 "...equally all objects of experience which are false harrass (them) with the poison of doubt." Tucci, Giuseppe; op. cit., p. 206. But cf. "yul" p. 43 above, (verse 12).

4 See p. 32 above, (verse 8). It must be said that Bhattacharya's editing of Tibetan leaves a lot to be desired when it comes to less important detail. In his transliteration "gśin rjeḥi" should be read for his "gśen rjeḥi".

5 See p. 42 above, (verse 10).

6 I.e. genitive singular "yakṣasya".

7 See: Staël-Holstein, Alexander August von; The Kāçyapaparivarta, Shanghai, 1926, SS 67, p. 100 f. This is quoted by Sthiramati, see: Yamaguchi, Susumu; Sthiramati : Madhyāntavibhāgaṭīkā : exposition systématique du Yogācāravijñaptivāda, Nagoya, 1934, vol. 1, p. 246. In Yamaguchi's manuscript "kṣaya" is found but in editing he amends that to "yakṣa". The quotation is also found in a commentary on the Āścarya-caryācaya, see: Haraprasad *Śāstri*; Bauddhagāna o dohā, Kalikātā, 1323 [1916], p. 6.

"After false imagining they are burned in hell and so on,
They burn by their faults, like bamboo on fire."[1]

In the Sanskrit and Chinese this follows the verse mentioning "great suffering in hell", and is connected but out of place.

Conjuring provides further similes dotted about in these versions:

"When a conjurer brings his trick to a conclusion after performing it,
It no longer exists that is the inherent nature of phenomena."[2]

And, coincidentally leading into our next topic:

"Sentient beings enjoy sense objects much as they would a conjurer's trick,
They encounter an illusory state of existence, materialised through dependent origination."[3]

1 See p. 41 above, (verse 8).
2 See p. 45 above, (verse 18).
3 See p. 42 above, (verse 9).

The Verses on the Heart of Dependent Origination (Pratītyasamutpāda-hṛdayakārikā) are attributed to Nāgārjuna in Chinese and Tibetan versions.[1]

Turning to the concept of dependent origination itself, Louis de La Vallée Poussin's Théorie des douze causes[2] is certainly without equal among pioneering works of western scholarship concerned with the concept. It remains valuable as an overview, though of course it is an early source. The textual material he provides reflects his wide-ranging approach to the study of Buddhism, including as it does the Śālistamba Sūtra, and extracts from the Daśabhūmika Sūtra, the Abhidharmakośa and the Candramahāroṣaṇa Tantra. Most importantly in the present context, La Vallée Poussin also edited and translated the Tibetan text of the Pratītyasamutpādahṛdayakārikā in the book.[3]

Ullaṅgha's Pratītyasamutpādaśastra is another text on dependent origination but is particularly significant in the present context because five of its thirty verses match the first five verses of our Pratītyasamutpāda-hṛdayakārikā. Vasudev Gokhale had worked on Ullaṅgha's text,[4] and this later led him into work on Nāgārjuna's Pratītyasamutpādahṛdayakārikā and

1 Doubt about this attribution is strongly held in Carmen Dragonetti's The Pratītyasamutpādahṛdayakārikā and the Pratītyasamutpādahṛdayavyākhyāna of Śuddhamati, *WZKS*, Wien : 1978; 22: 87–93, inspired by Vasudev Gokhale's opinion that Śuddhamati was the author of the Pratītyasamutpādahṛdayavyākhyāna. (Gokhale, Vasudev; Pratītyasamutpādaśastra des Ullaṅgha kritisch behandelt und aus dem Chinesischen ins Deutsche übertragen, Bonn, 1930, p. 6.) For a critical treatment of Dragonetti's "Śuddhamati" see: Lindtner, Christian; Adversaria Buddhica, *WZKS*, Wien : 1982; 26: 167–172. The most recent stage of this debate can be found in Carmen Dragonetti's On Śuddhamati's Pratītyasamutpādahṛdaya-kārikā and on Bodhicittavivaraṇa, *WZKS*, Wien : 1986; 30: 109–122.

2 Gand, 1913.

3 Op. cit., p. 122–124.

4 Gokhale, Vasudev; op. cit. *and also* Gokhale, Vasudev; Eine der im Sanskrittext verloren gegangenen buddhistischen Sūtren aus dem Chinesischen übertragen, *Chinesisch-deutscher Almanach für das Jahr 1930*, Frankfurt am Main : 1930; p. 61–75.

its commentary.[1]

A translation of Ullangha's Pratītyasamutpādaśastra is available in his "Eine der im Sanskrittext verloren gegangenen buddhistischen Sūtren aus dem Chinesischen übertragen", a translation taking as its source Dharmagupta's Chinese translation of the text. The verses which correspond to the first five verses of our Pratītyasamutpādahṛdayakārikā are 26, 6, 27, 28 and 30.

Gokhale's "Der Sanskrit-Text von Nāgārjuna's Pratītyasamutpāda-hṛdayakārikā" was the result of his discovery of a Sanskrit manuscript almost twenty years later in 1949 in the Kun bde gling monastery in Lhasa,[2] a manuscript which also had within its contents a quotation of these five verses, with commentary for the first three verses. Clearly part of the text of the commentary is not there, though the manuscript continues with another work on dependent origination. Gokhale provides us with an edition of the five Sanskrit verses and the part of the commentary contained in his manuscript. There is no title provided by the manuscript, but he himself provisionally entitles the text of the complete manuscript Tīrthyamatalakṣaṇanirākaraṇam.[3] Though the Lhasa manuscript is not easily available, Gokhale provided me with a photocopy of his transcript. Upon examination the variants are found not to amount to anything out of the ordinary — simply matters of punctuation, consistency and the tidying up of case endings. Nevertheless it is helpful to see where there is speculation in readings and where there have been emendations.

Gokhale makes the assumption that only the first five verses of our seven verse Pratītyasamutpādahṛdayakārikā — the five verses he has in his Lhasa manuscript — are Nāgārjuna's,[4] a view which Aiyaswami Sastri adopts.[5] L. Jamspal and Peter della Santina's opinion is that the two verses are

1 Gokhale, Vasudev; Der Sanskrit-Text von Nāgārjuna's Pratītyasamutpādahṛdaya-kārikā, p. 101–106 in: Studia Indologica. Festschrift für Willibald Kirfel zur Vollendung seines 70. Lebensjahres, (Bonner Orientaliche Studien, Neue Serie ; 3), Bonn, 1955; and also: Gokhale, Vasudev; Encore: the Pratītyasamutpādahṛdayakārikā of Nāgārjuna, p. 62–68 (with plates) in: Dhadphale, M. G.; Principal V. S. Apte commemoration volume, Poona, 1978.

2 See his p. 102. Gokhale was a Government of India representative at Lhasa from 1948 to 1950.

3 Ibid., p. 103.

4 Ibid., p. 101 n. 2.

5 Aiyaswami Sastri, N.; Nagarjuna's exposition of twelve causal links, *Bulletin of Tibetology*, Gangtok : 1968; 5(2): p. 10.

certainly later additions.[1] Dragonetti follows this line of thinking by asserting that the original Sanskrit text had only the first five verses,[2] and this is a conclusion which Lindtner supports.[3] The last two verses of our text certainly give the appearance of being tagged on to the end in our commentary, the Pratītyasamutpādahṛdayavyākhyāna. Probably the most devastating point made against any possibility of there being one original text of seven verses is Aiyaswami Sastri's comment that the first five verses were in ārya metre while the last two were in anuṣṭubh metre.[4] The evidence pointed out in all the sources is overwhelming, but my translation persists in presenting the text in seven verses as found in the Tibetan tradition.

A minor point is that, against Gokhale's assumption, the sixth verse can still be Nāgārjuna's if it is accepted as essentially the same as verse 12 of Nāgārjuna's Yuktiṣaṣṭikākārikā;[5] it just is not a part of the Pratītya-samutpādahṛdayakārikā. Turning next to the seventh verse — and borrowing Takasaki's comment in his work on the Ratnagotravibhāga — it is such a "widely applicable idea" that it need not be regarded "as a quotation from any particular source."[6] Such a verse can be encountered almost anywhere.

Most importantly Gokhale's first editing of the Sanskrit has been superseded by his second editing in the light of another manuscript, in collaboration with M. G. Dhadpale,[7] M. G. Dhadpale was working on a manuscript which turned out to contain on three of its folios the Pratītyasamutpādahṛdayakārikā and an incomplete version of the

1 Jamspal, L.; The Pratītyasamutpāda-hṛdaya-kārikā-vyākhyāna of Nāgārjuna, reconstruction and translation into English from the Tibetan, *Buddhist studies. A yearly research journal of the Department of Buddhist Studies, University of Delhi,* Delhi : 1974; 1: p. 10.

2 Dragonetti, Carmen; op. cit., p. 90.

3 Lindtner, Christian; op. cit., p. 167.

4 Aiyaswami Sastri, N.; op. cit., p. 5 and 10. There is of course no extant Sanskrit version of verse six other than as a reconstruction, but Aiyaswami Sastri's speculation does not seem too far-fetched. At least verse seven can be found extant in Sanskrit in anuṣṭubh metre.

5 See p. 51 above. Gokhale could not really have been expected to foresee such a possibility when he rejected Nāgārjuna's authorship.

6 Takasaki, Jikido; op. cit., p. 301. Cf. p. 52 above, (verse 7).

7 Gokhale, Vasudev; Encore: the Pratītyasamutpādahṛdayakārikā of Nāgārjuna, p. 62–68 (with plates) in: Dhadphale, M. G.; Principal V. S. Apte commemoration volume, Poona, 1978.

Pratītyasamutpādahṛdayavyākhyāna. Once more the Sanskrit available is incomplete but this manuscript is considerably more complete than Gokhale's Lhasa manuscript used for his earlier edition. Rather than the five verses of Gokhale's Lhasa manuscript this version contains six verses, the last corresponding to the seventh verse in our Pratītyasamutpādahṛdaya-kārikā. This 'new' manuscript is among the Gilgit manuscripts removed from Kashmir in 1947 to the National Archives of the Government of India in New Delhi. Until P. V. Bapat's interest in these manuscripts it was possible only to examine them there; no public communications about their contents could be made. Bapat managed to have this restriction, which had been imposed by the Government of Kashmir, lifted. He then published a list of the manuscripts in his "Gilgit manuscripts and numerical symbols".[1] In that list number 59, Prasenajit-gāthā, contained more than that text alone, and among other texts it included the Pratītyasamutpādahṛdayakārikā and the incomplete version of the Pratītyasamutpādahṛdayavyākhyāna which provide the source for Gokhale's second editing of the Sanskrit texts. In Gokhale's article the manuscript is edited, the final missing part reconstructed, and reproductions of the photographs of the manuscript are provided in the plates.

Lindtner, in his Adversaria Buddhica, has also provided us with edited versions of our first five verses in Sanskrit, in the Tibetan translation of the Sanskrit and in the Chinese translation of the Tibetan.[2] He further provides the quotation in Tibetan from Bhavya's Prajñāpradīpa giving a prose version of our fifth verse, followed by the quotation in Tibetan from Bhavya's Madhyamakaratnapradīpa giving a metrical version of verses two through six.[3] The latter quotation, though it is not always identical with our Tibetan, is certainly a quotation of the very same verses.

Sanskrit quotations of the Pratītyasamutpādahṛdayakārikā are also available for some of the verses. The second half of verse four is quoted twice in Prajñākaramati's Bodhicaryāvatārapañjikā. It is also quoted in the Pañcakrama. It is also quoted in Kambalapāda's Navaślokī. Verse five is quoted twice in Candrakīrti's Prasannapadā Madhyamakavṛtti.[4]

1 *Journal of the Oriental Institute, Maharaja Sayajirao University of Baroda*, Baroda : 1961; 11: 127–131.

2 Lindtner, Christian; op. cit., p. 169 f.

3 Ibid. p. 168 f.

4 Specific references are given with the appropriate edited Tibetan verses above. See p. 49 (footnote to verse 4) and p. 50 (footnote to verse 5).

An Explanation of the Heart of Dependent Origination (Pratītyasamutpāda-hṛdayavyākhyāna) is attributed to Nāgārjuna in Chinese and Tibetan versions. Lindtner, on grounds of style, clearly doubts the soundness of this attribution.[1]

One substantial translating team is mentioned for our Tibetan translations of the text, namely Jinamitra, Dānaśīla, Śīlendrabodhi, Ye shes sde, and other unnamed translators and revisors.[2] This team may be ultimately responsible for all of the Tibetan translations in the canon of both the Pratītyasamutpādahṛdayakārikā and the Pratītyasamutpādahṛdaya-vyākhyāna, but we can at least attach them to the first canonical versions[3] of the Pratītyasamutpādahṛdayavyākhyāna with considerable certainty. It seems unlikely that there were two separate translation teams, as there was with the Mahāyānaviṃśikā, especially in view of the much closer correspondence between the first and second translations. It would seem that all versions of our Tibetan translations could stem from the same Sanskrit manuscript or manuscripts in the hands of the translators, something which is altogether inconceivable in the case of the Mahāyānaviṃśikā.

N. Aiyaswami Sastri provided a translation of the Chinese version of the Pratītyasamutpādahṛdayavyākhyāna.[4] Later Gokhale, as mentioned above,[5] edited the Sanskrit versions of the commentary found in his Sanskrit manuscripts, substantially matching our Tibetan commentary, though variations from his editions are too numerous to document in footnotes to

1 Lindtner, Christian; op. cit., p. 172. Dragonetti mentions an attribution to Sthiramati, Dragonetti, Carmen; op. cit., p. 92.

2 This team of translators can be reliably placed in the ninth century and each one is known to have worked on a number of texts, often working together in various combinations. Jinamitra and this particular Dānaśīla are both Kashmiri translators. Śīlendrabodhi is probably a Kashmiri and is certainly a translator in the ninth century. Ye shes sde is one of the principal Tibetan translators of the time. (See: Naudou, Jean, op. cit., p. 86–90.)

3 I.e. "first" in their order in the bstan 'gyur, generally dbu ma 17 (tsa) as opposed to dbu ma 33 (gi).

4 Aiyaswami Sastri, N.; Nāgārjuna on the Buddhist theory of causation, p. 485–491 in the: Professor K. V. Rangaswami Aiyangar commemoration volume, Madras, 1940. His source was Taishō No. 1654.

5 See p. 77 f. above.

my Tibetan edition. Instead those editions should be consulted by way of comparison. In the development of work on the text there lies — between Gokhale's two editions — Aiyaswami Sastri's Sanskrit version of the Pratītyasamutpādahṛdayakārikā with its Pratītyasamutpādahṛdayavyākhyāna, based upon Gokhale's first edition, while reconstructing what was missing and also editing the Tibetan.[1] His Sanskrit follows Gokhale exactly for the first five verses in the Pratītyasamutpādahṛdayakārikā, while in the Pratītyasamutpādahṛdayavyākhyāna he takes the Tibetan and Chinese into account for his reconstruction, even for the parts which Gokhale's Sanskrit manuscript covers. Gokhale's important second editing of the Sanskrit text came out in that same year and inevitably carries more weight as a new edition of the Sanskrit in the light of a more complete manuscript.

L. Jamspal and Peter della Santina provided an English translation and a Sanskrit reconstruction of the Pratītyasamutpādahṛdayavyākhyāna based on the Tibetan.[2] Which edition or editions of the Tibetan were used is not stated. Their article is a readable and very careful piece of work achieving what it sets out to do: taking a Tibetan version of the text, translating it into English and reconstructing a Sanskrit version from the Tibetan.

Yūichi Kajiyama has provided an edition of the Tibetan text of the Pratītyasamutpādahṛdayavyākhyāna based on the Tibetan canonical versions in the light of the Chinese text from Dunhuang in an article on the Tibetan "Commentary on the Heart of Dependent Origination" which appeared in a Japanese Buddhist Society monograph on issues of life and death in Buddhism.[3] His work is interesting and valuable but not always accurate. It would have been unnecessary for me to provide a detailed edition of the canonical versions of this text if my variant readings could have been confined to the occasional mention in a footnote. However, by way of example, of the first thirty footnotes of variant readings he provides in his article twenty do not agree with my readings. That ratio does not change very much throughout the text. This odd variation between readings is most striking for the sNar thang edition of the canon. Even where it is certain we

1 Aiyaswami Sastri, N.; Nagarjuna's exposition of twelve causal links, *Bulletin of Tibetology*, Gangtok : 1968; 5(2): 5–27.

2 The Pratītyasamutpāda-hṛdaya-kārikā-vyākhyāna of Nāgārjuna, reconstruction and translation into English from the Tibetan, *Buddhist studies. A yearly research journal of the Department of Buddhist Studies, University of Delhi,* Delhi : 1974; 1: [9]-24.

3 Kajiyama, Yūichi; Zōbon "Innen shinron shaku", p. 1–15 in: Bukkyō ni okeru seishi no mondai, Kyōto, 1981.

are both using exactly the same source (and not printed texts of an edition produced from blocks at different times) — namely the Co ne edition where we both use the Institute for Advanced Study of World Religions' microfiche — we are not always in agreement.

Kajiyama collates the Tibetan using as his sources Peking, Co ne, sDe dge and sNar thang editions of the canon. He provides two sets of footnotes, the first providing variant readings and the second providing comparison between Gokhale's Sanskrit, the canonical Tibetan and the Dunhuang Chinese. In places helpful reconstructed Sanskrit phrases accompany Tibetan readings. These second seventy-three footnotes present much that is of interest. Kajiyama does not make use of the Dunhuang Tibetan texts.

A much more modern copy of the Pratītyasamutpādahṛdayakārikā and the Pratītyasamutpādahṛdayavyākhyāna is available among the Tibetan manuscripts and xylographs in the Sándor Kőrösi Csoma collection in the library of the Hungarian Academy of Sciences (Magyar Tudományos Akadémia), Budapest. The collection was given by Csoma to his student S. C. Malan in 1839 and he gave it to the Hungarian Academy of Sciences in 1884.

The manuscript is now numbered 1 in the collection.[1] In Malan's own list it had been numbered XXII.[2]

Csoma 1 is a manuscript in pothī format written on Tibetan paper. It consists of three folios and measures 7.6 x 51.5 cm. There are eight lines of writing on each side of the folios. The writing is dbu med.[3] The manuscript begins with the Pratītyasamutpādahṛdayakārikā which is followed by the Pratītyasamutpādahṛdayavyākhyāna. It is of some interest, but with regard to the editing of the two texts it must be treated as a relatively modern copy of canonical versions.

1 See: Terjék, József; Collection of Tibetan mss. and xylographs of Alexander Csoma de Körös, Budapest, 1976, p. 19 for an up-to-date catalogue entry for the manuscript. An earlier catalogue entry is available in Nagy, Louis J.; Tibetan books and manuscripts of Alexander Csoma de Kőrös in the library of the Hungarian Academy of Sciences, p. 29–56 in: Ligeti, Lajos; Analecta Orientalia memoriae Alexandri Csoma de Kőrös, Budapestini, 1942.

2 Malan, Solomon Caesar; Tibetan books and manuscripts of the late Alexander Csoma de Körös presented to the Royal Hungarian Academy of Sciences at Budapest, *JRAS. N.S.*, London : 1884; 16: 494.

3 Headless.

Among Dunhuang manuscripts there is much to be found which is of considerable editorial interest. Among further sources for both the Pratītyasamutpādahṛdayavyākhyāna and indirectly for the Pratītyasamutpādahṛdayakārikā are the Stein collection manuscripts from Dunhuang now in the India Office Library within the British Library in London. The relevant items for Tibetan material are Stein 621, 622, 623 and 624.[1] Also among further sources for the Pratītyasamutpādahṛdayakārikā itself and the Pratītyasamutpādahṛdayavyākhyāna are the Pelliot collection manuscripts from Dunhuang now in the Bibliothèque Nationale in Paris. The relevant items for Tibetan material are Pelliot tibétain Touen-houang 114A, 762, 763, 764, 765, 766, 768 and 769.[2] These manuscripts are edited and considered in part three below and played a full part in the translation in part one above. The Chinese material[3] has been considered by Hakuju Ui in his study of Buddhist texts from Dunhuang.[4]

* * * * *

1 See: La Vallée Poussin, Louis de; Catalogue of the Tibetan manuscripts from Tunhuang in the India Office Library, London, 1962, p. 194 f.

2 See: Lalou, Marcelle; Inventaire des manuscrits tibétains de Touen-houang conservés à la Bibliothèque Nationale, (Fonds Pelliot n°s 1–849), Paris, 1939, p. 38 and p. 167 f.

3 Serial numbers 5815, 5816 and 5819 corresponding to Stein numbers 1358, 2462 and 269 respectively, see: Giles, Lionel; Descriptive catalogue of the Chinese manuscripts from Tunhuang in the British Museum, London, 1957.

4 Ui, Hakuju; Engi shinju no zōkō hatten, p. 235–271 in his Seiiki Butten no kenkyū, Tōkyō, 1969.

Part 3

Dunhuang texts

Preface

The English translation of Nāgārjuna's Pratītyasamutpādahṛdayakārikā with the Pratītyasamutpādahṛdayavyākhyāna — found in part one of this study — and its critical study accompanied by an edited version of the Tibetan texts — found in part two of this study — is complemented by part three which includes a critical study accompanied by an edited version of the relevant Tibetan texts found at Dunhuang : the Pratītyasamutpāda-hṛdayakārikā, the Pratītyasamutpādahṛdayavyākhyāna and the Pratītya-samutpādahṛdayavyākhyānābhismaraṇa.

Verses on the Heart of Dependent Origination[1]

(taken from a Dunhuang manuscript)

[2]rgya gar skad du /

pra ti tya sa mud pa’ da’ hri da ya ka ri ka //

bod skad du

rten cing ’brel pa’r ’byung ba’i snying po / tshig le’ur byas pa’(Pelliot mss) //

’jam dpal gzho nur[3] gyur pa la phyag ’tshal lo //

1 Pelliot tibétain Touen-houang 769. Folio 1a-1b.
2 Pelliot 769 begins here.
3 I.e. “gzhon nur”. Use of abbreviation is common in Tibetan texts from Dunhuang.

yan lag bye brag bcu gnyis gang //
thub pas rten byung gsungs de dag /
nyon mongs las dang sdug bsngal dang //
gsum po dag tu zad par 'dus // [1]

dang po brgyad dang dgu nyon mongs //
gnyis dang bcu pa[1] las yin te //
lhag ma' bdun yang sdug bsngal yin //
bcu gnyis chos ni gsum du 'dus // [2]

gsum po dag las gnyis 'byung ste //
gnyis las bdun 'byung bdun las kyang //
gsum 'byung srid pa' 'khor lo de //
nyid ni yang dang yang du 'khor // [3]

'gro kun rgyu dang 'bras bu ste //
'di la sems can gzhan ji yang myed[2] //[3]
stong pa kho na'i chos rnams las //
stong pa'i chos rnams 'byung bar zad // [4]

kha ton mar mye mye long rgya //
mye shel sa bon skyur dang sgras //
phung po'i nying mtshams[4] sbyor ba dang[5] //
myi 'pho bar yang mkhas[6] rtogs bya // [5]

1 Pelliot 769 adds a "dang" here but both letters are marked for deletion with small ticks above them.

2 Spellings with "ya btags" in forms like this are common in Tibetan texts from Dunhuang.

3 Note that there is an extra syllable in this line in Pelliot 769 causing the line not to fit the metre. Presumably "ji yang" was pronounced as one syllable.

4 In Pelliot 769 the flag on the "tsha" of "mtshams" rises from the centre of the letter, not the right end and looks like a tick used to mark letters for deletion.

5 Consistently "yang" in canonical versions.

6 In Pelliot 769 the "ma" of "mkhas" is added below the line, and marked with a caret.

shin tu phra ba'i dngos la yang //
gang gis chad par rnam brtags pa' //
rnam par myi mkhas de yis ni //
rkyen las byung ba'i don ma mthong //[1] [6]

'di [la bsal bya][2] gang yang myed //
gzhag par bya ba' ji yang myed //
yang dag nyid la yang dag lta //
yang dag mthong na' rnam par grol // [7]

//[3] rten cing 'brel par 'byung ba'i snying po tshig le'ur byas pa' // slobs dpon klus bsgrub kyis mdzad pa rdzogs so /[4]

1 Cf. the similar verse 12 of Nāgārjuna's Yuktiṣaṣṭikākārikā available among Dunhuang manuscripts, namely Pelliot 796:

"shin tu phra ba'i dngos la yang //
gang gis skye bar rnam brtags pa' //
rnam par myi mkhas de yis ni //
rkyen las byung ba'i don ma mthong //

(Verse cited by Cristina Scherrer-Schaub in her: Un manuscrit tibétain des Pratītyasamutpādahṛdayakārikā de Nāgārjuna, *Cahiers d' Extrême-Asia*, Kyōto : 1987; 3: 108 n. 42.)

2 Pelliot 769 does not have the expected " 'di la bsal bya" but instead " 'di las / ba". The reading here is quite odd and does not fit the metre. The line has a large red blot marking the beginning of serious error. A proofreader or teacher rejecting the folio perhaps?

3 In Pelliot 769 this double shad is preceded by a high "zhabs kyu" like symbol and a tsheg.

4 Pelliot 769 ends here.

An Interpretation of the Heart of Dependent Origination[1]

(taken from Dunhuang manuscripts)

[2]rgya gar [3] skad du /

[4]pra ti' tya sa mud pa' da hri da ya [5]bya khya na[6] [7]/[8]/

1 Pelliot tibétain Touen-houang 114A (Folio 1a-1b), 762 (Panels 1–5), 763 (Folio 2a-2b), 764 (Folio 1a-1b), 765 (Folio 2a-2b), 766 (Folio 1a-2b), 768 (Folio 4a-4b), Stein 620 (Tibetan MSS Tun Huang Collection Volume 4, Catalogue number 620, Original number Ch.51.I.31, Folios 69a-69b, [MS 595]), 621.1 (Tibetan MSS Tun Huang Collection Volume 4, Catalogue number 621.1, Original numbers Ch.51.I.8 [47] and Ch.73.VII.9, Folios 70a-73a (70a-70b Ch.51.I.8 [47] and 71a-73a Ch.73.VII.9), [MS 596]), 623 (Tibetan MSS Tun Huang Collection Volume 4, Catalogue number 623, Original number Ch.51.I.11 [50], Folios 81a-81b, [MS 598]) and 624 (Tibetan MSS Tun Huang Collection Volume 32, Catalogue number 624, Original number Ch.73.XV fragment 10a, Folios 67a-67b, [MS 599]) are edited here. Stein 621.2 and 622 follow.

2 Pelliot 114A, 763, 765 and Stein 623 begin here. Note that extensive interlinear text is found in Pelliot 763 and Stein 623. Throughout Pelliot 765 almost all black shads are doubled with a shadowing red shad, following or before.

3 Pelliot 763 adds "gyi" here. Pelliot 114A, 765 and Stein 623 omit it.

4 Pelliot 762 begins here and — based on the size of the gaps in the text on the lines below it — it looks more or less certain a Sanskrit title was included to the left when the folio was whole. Note that extensive interlinear text is found in Pelliot 762.

5 Pelliot 766 begins here. Note that extensive interlinear text is found in Pelliot 766.

6 Pelliot 114A has "pra ti tya sa mud pa' da' hri da ya bya khya' na". Pelliot 762 has "pra ti tya sa mud ba' hri da ya' bya khya' na". Pelliot 763 has "pra ti tya / sa mud ba' da' hri da' bya' khya' na". Pelliot 765 has "pra ti tya / sa mud pa' da hri da ya' bya' khya' na'". Stein 623 has "pra ti' tya sa mud pa' da hri da ya bya khya na" Pelliot 766 has "bya khya' na".

7 Pelliot 764 begins here.

8 Pelliot 764 adds the occasional extra red shad in its punctuation, including a fancy zig zag red shad here.

bod skad du //

rten cing 'brel par[1] 'byung ba'i[2] snying po[3]
rnam par bshad pa[4] //

'jam dpal[5] gzhonur[6] gyur[7] [8]pa [9] la phyag 'tshal[10] lo //

1 Pelliot 114A has " 'brel par 'brel par" for " 'brel par" and each character of the first " 'brel par" is ticked with a red tick. Pelliot 762, 763, 764, 765 and Stein 623 have " 'brel par". Pelliot 766 has " 'brel bar"

2 In Pelliot 766 " 'byung bar" precedes " 'byung ba'i", presumably an error which was not marked or crossed out.

3 Pelliot 114A, 762, 763, 764, 766 and Stein 623 "snying po". Pelliot 765 "snying".

4 Pelliot 763 and Stein 623 "bshad pa". Pelliot 114A, 762, 764, 765 and 766 "bshad pa'".

5 Pelliot 114A, 763, 764, 765, 766 and Stein 623 " 'jam dpal". Pelliot 762 " 'jaṃ dpal" with a "pa" written in error and crossed out between the " 'a chung" and the "ja".

6 Pelliot 114A, 762, 763, 764, 765 and 766 "gzho nur". Stein 623 "gzhonur", i.e. "gzhon nur".

7 Pelliot 114A, 762, 763, 764, 765 and 766 "gyur". Stein 623 "gyurd". Da drag is common in Tibetan texts from Dunhuang.

8 Pelliot 762 is missing the following.

9 In Pelliot 766 something has been erased here.

10 Pelliot 114A, 763, 764, 766 and Stein 623 " 'tshal". Pelliot 765 " 'tsal".

'[1]di la dge [2]sbyong[3] nyan 'dod pa[4] [5]mnyan pa[6] dang / gzung ba [7]dang / khong du chud par[8] bya ba[9] dang / [10]rtog pa dang / sel nus pa[11] dang ldan ba'i[12] slob ma zhig / slob dpon [13]gyi[14] gan du 'ongs nas / de

1 Pelliot 762 recommences.

2 Pelliot 764 is missing the following.

3 Pelliot 114A, 762, 763, 766 and Stein 623 "sbyong". Pelliot 766 "sbyongs", though the "sa" is very faint indeed and may have been scratched away. In Pelliot 762 "sbyong" is preceded by a "ba" which has not been crossed out or marked for deletion.

4 Pelliot 114A, 762, 763, 765 and Stein 623 " 'dod pa". Pelliot 766 " 'dod pas". The "pa" of " 'dod pa" in Pelliot 763 appears in one line with a mark for deletion and then is repeated on the next line, presumably a second thought about how much space needed to be left for interlinear text.

5 Pelliot 766 is missing the following.

6 Pelliot 765 omits "mnyan pa". Pelliot 114A, 762, 763 and Stein 623 have it.

7 Pelliot 766 recommences.

8 Pelliot 763, 114A, 765, 766 and Stein 623 "chud par". Pelliot 762 "cud par".

9 Pelliot 114A, 762, 763, 765 and Stein 623 "bya ba". Pelliot 766 "bya ba'"

10 Pelliot 764 recommences.

11 Pelliot 114A, 762, 764, 765, 766 and Stein 623 "sel nus pa". Pelliot 763 has "sel nus pa'i", but the gi gu has been crossed out.

12 Pelliot 114A, 762, 763, 764, 765, 766 and Stein 623 have "ldan ba'i", not "ldan pa'i".

13 Pelliot 762 is missing the following.

14 Pelliot 114A "slob dpon gyi". (Pelliot 762 "slobs dpon".) Pelliot 763 and 765 "slobs dpon gyi". Pelliot 764 "slobs dpon gi". Pelliot 766 and Stein 623 "slobs dpon kyi", reflecting "da drag", i.e. not "slobs dpon gyi" even though no final "d" is represented in the orthography.

bzhin gshegs pa'i [1]bstan pa las[2] brtsams te[3] / 'di skad 'dri[4] 'o //[5] [6]bcom ldan 'das[7] [8] 'di la [9] //[10] « *yan lag bye brag bcu gnyis gang // thub pa*[11]*s rten*[12] *'byung*[13] *gsungs de dag /* » [14] gang du bsdu bar blta ba[15] [16] thos par[17] 'tshal lo //[18]

de [19] chos de dag gi[20] de kho na[21] nyid 'dri bar[22] [23]rig nas // [24]slob dpon

1 Pelliot 762 recommences.

2 Pelliot 763, 764, 765 and Stein 623 "las". In Pelliot 765 something has been erased between "las" and "brtsams". Pelliot 114A and 766 "la". Pelliot 762 "da la /" but "da" has been crossed out, or else it is "de" with a " 'greng bu" which went a little astray.

3 Pelliot 114A, 764, 765, 766 and Stein 623 "brtsams te". Pelliot 762 and 763 "brtsam ste".

4 Pelliot 764 is missing the following.

5 Pelliot 766 is unclear as much has been scraped off.

6 Pelliot 766 is missing the following.

7 Pelliot 114A, 762, 763 and 765 "bcom ldan 'das". Stein 623 "bcom ldan 'da's".

8 Pelliot 765 adds "la" here. Pelliot 114A, 762, 763 and Stein 623 omit it.

9 Pelliot 762 is missing the following.

10 Pelliot 766 recommences.

11 Pelliot 764 recommences.

12 Pelliot 763, 765 and 766 "*rten*". Pelliot 114A, 764 and Stein 623 "b*rten*".

13 Pelliot 114A, 764, 765, 766 and Stein 623 " '*byung*". Pelliot 763 "*byung*".

14 Text found between these chevrons or guillemets français appears in red ink in the manuscripts.

15 Pelliot 763, 764, 765, 766 and Stein 623 "bsdu bar blta ba". Pelliot 114A "bsdu' bar blta' ba".

16 Pelliot 764 adds "de" here. Pelliot 114A, 763, 765, 766 and Stein 623 omit it.

17 Pelliot 114A, 763, 765, 766 and Stein 623 "thos par". Pelliot 764 "thob par".

18 This double shad appears as black shad, red shad, two vertical double circles red inside black, red shad, black shad, red shad, two vertical double circles red inside black, red shad, black shad in Pelliot 114A. Pelliot 766 has a single shad. Pelliot 763, 765 and Stein 623 have a double shad. Pelliot 764 has a triple shad.

19 In Pelliot 764 there is virtually a shad between "de" and "chos". Pelliot 114A, 763, 765, 766 and Stein 623 omit it.

20 Pelliot 114A, 763, 765, 766 and Stein "gi". Pelliot 764 omits it.

21 In Pelliot 114A a "kha" precedes the "de kho na", as if the "kho" was begun prematurely, but it is marked in black at the top as if to be crossed out. Pelliot 763, 764 and Stein 623 "de kho na". Pelliot 765 "kho na". Pelliot 766 "de kho na'".

22 In Pelliot 766 the "ra" of "bar" is inserted below the line.

23 Pelliot 762 recommences.

24 Pelliot 764 and 766 are missing the following.

gyis[1] 'di skad ces[2] bu //[3] [4]« *nyon mongs las dang sdug bsngal dang /*[5]*/ gsum po dag du zad par 'dus //* »

shes gsal[6] zhing zur pḥyin [7]pa'i[8] tshig[9] 'di[10] smras so // de la bcu dang[11] gnyis ni [12] bcu gnyis so[13] /[14]/ yan [15]lag rnams [16]nyid ni /[17] bye brag yin [18]bas[19] na // yan lag bye brag[20] ste / [21]shing rta'i[22] yan lag bzhin [23]du

1 Pelliot 114A "slob dpon gyis". Stein 623 "slobs dpon kyis". Pelliot 763, 765 "slobs dpon gyis". Pelliot 762 "slobs pon gis".

2 Pelliot 766 recommences.

3 In Pelliot 765 it would appear an attempt was made to write a few words here, then they were erased and extra shads were inserted to fill the gap.

4 Pelliot 762 is missing the following.

5 Pelliot 764 recommences.

6 Pelliot 114A, 763, 764 and 765 "gsal". Pelliot 766 "gstsal". In Stein 623 this is covered with tape and difficult to read. It is not "gsal" but it may be "gstsal".

7 Pelliot 762 recommences.

8 Pelliot 764, 765, 766 and Stein 623 "phyin pa'i". (Pelliot 762 "[phyin] pa'i".) Pelliot 114A "phyind pa'i". Pelliot 763 "phyin ba'i".

9 Pelliot 114A, 762, 763, 764, 766 and Stein 623 "tshig". Pelliot 765 "tshigs".

10 Pelliot 114A, 762, 763, 765, 766 and Stein 623 " 'di". In Pelliot 114A this " 'di" is added below the line, with a cross above the line, all in red ink. Pelliot 764 omits it.

11 Pelliot 114A, 763, 764, 765, 766 and Stein 623 "dang". Pelliot 762 omits it.

12 In Stein 623 something is written between "ni" and "bcu".

13 Pelliot 114A, 762, 763, 766 and Stein 623 "gnyis so". Pelliot 764 "gnyis so'". Pelliot 765 "gnyiso".

14 Pelliot 766 is missing the following.

15 Pelliot 764 is missing the following.

16 Pelliot 762 is missing the following.

17 Stein 623 "ni /". Pelliot 114A, 763 and 765 omit it.

18 Pelliot 766 recommences.

19 Pelliot 114A, 763, 765 and Stein 623 "yin bas", not "yin pas". (Pelliot 766 "bas".)

20 Pelliot 114A, 763, 766 and Stein 623 "bye brag". Pelliot 765 "bye breg".

21 Pelliot 762 recommences.

22 Pelliot 114A, 762, 765 and Stein 623 "shing rta'i". Pelliot 766 "shing rta".

23 Pelliot 764 recommences.

yan lag[1] du gyur pa[2] bstan to[3] // sku dang [4]gsung [5] thub pas na thub pa'o // thub pa des gsungs pa[6] zhes bya ba ni //[7] bstan pa[8] dang [9]bshad pa zhes bya ba'i[10] [11]rnam[12] [13]grangs su[14] gtogs pa'o[15] // de yang[16] rang bzhin dang / nges pa dang / skyes bu[17] dang / gzhan [18]la rag las pa[19] dang / dbang phyug[20] dang / dus dang / ngo bo nyid dang / 'dod rgyal[21] dang / gnam

1 In Pelliot 114A a "lag" precedes "yan lag" but both letters of the first "lag" are marked in black at the top as if to be crossed out. In Pelliot 762 an extra "yan lag" precedes "yan lag" but it has been crossed out.

2 Pelliot 762 and 764 "gyur pa". Pelliot 114A, 763 and Stein 623 "gyurd pa". Pelliot 765 " 'gyurd pa'". Pelliot 766 "gyur pa' /".

3 Pelliot 762, 763, 764, 765 and Stein 623 "bstan to". Pelliot 765 looks like once had a letter between the "ta" and "na" of "bstan", perhaps "ta". Pelliot 114A "bstand to". Pelliot 766 "bstan tho".

4 In Pelliot 766 a "thu" precedes this "gsung" but has been crossed out.

5 Pelliot 114A, 762, 763, 764, 765, 766 and Stein 623 omit the expected "dang thugs".

6 Pelliot 114A, 762, 764, 765, 766 and Stein 623 "gsungs pa". Pelliot 763 "gsungs". Pelliot 114A ends here.

7 In Pelliot 763 the writing of these last two phrases is quite unnaturally stretched out.

8 Pelliot 762, 763, 764, 766 and Stein 623 "bstan pa". Pelliot 765 "bstan ba".

9 Pelliot 766 is missing the following.

10 Pelliot 763, 764 and Stein 623 "zhes bya ba'i". Pelliot 762 "shes bya ba'i". Pelliot 765 "zhes bya ba ni".

11 Pelliot 764 is missing the following.

12 Pelliot 762, 763 and Stein 623 "rnam". Pelliot 765 "rnams".

13 Pelliot 766 recommences.

14 Pelliot 762, 763, 765 and Stein 623 "grangs su". Pelliot 766 abbreviates this to "grangsu".

15 Pelliot 762, 765, 766 and Stein 623 "gtogs pa'o". Pelliot 763 "gthogs pa'o".

16 In Pelliot 766 the "nga" of "yang" is written below the line.

17 In Pelliot 765 something has been erased from between the "skyes" and "bu" of "skyes bu".

18 Pelliot 764 recommences.

19 Pelliot 763, 764, 765, 766 and Stein 623 "rag las pa". Pelliot 762 "rag lus pa".

20 Pelliot 762, 763, 765, 766 and Stein 623 "dbang phyug". Pelliot 764 "dbang phyung".

21 Pelliot 763, 765, 766 and Stein 623 " 'dod rgyal". Pelliot 762 "mdod rgyal".

gyis[1] bskos [2] pa dang / gyi na la stsogs pa'i[3] rgyu rnams las [4]byung ba ni ma[5] yin te[6] // de ni rten cing 'brel par 'byung ba'o[7] // yan lag [8] bye brag bcu [9]gnyis po 'di[10] dag ni / nyon mongs pa dang / las dang[11] /[12] sdug bsngal rnams su[13] gcig la gcig[14] rten[15] te // mdung khyim[16] gyi[17] tshul[18] du gsum po[19] [20]dag du zad [21]par 'dus par 'gyur ro /[22]/ zad par zhes bya ba ni

1 Pelliot 763, 765 and Stein 623 "gnam gyis". Pelliot 766 "gnam kyis". Pelliot 762 and 764 "gnam gis".

2 Pelliot 763 adds a "ba" here with no sign of it being marked or crossed out. Pelliot 762, 764, 765, 766 and Stein 623 omit it.

3 I.e. "la sogs pa'i". Pelliot 764, 765 and Stein 623 "la stsogs pa'i". Pelliot 762 "la stsogs pa". Pelliot 766 "las stsogs pa'i". Pelliot 763 "la bstsogs pa'i".

4 Pelliot 762 has something like "stsa" in front of "byung ba" but it has been crossed out.

Pelliot 764 is missing the following.

5 In Pelliot 765 a "ya" was begun before "ma", but was never marked or crossed out.

6 Pelliot 762, 763, 765 and Stein 623 "yin te". Pelliot 766 "yin the".

7 Pelliot 762, 763, 766 and Stein 623 " 'byung ba'o". Pelliot 765 " 'byung bo".

8 Pelliot 765 adds "dang" here. Pelliot 762, 763, 766 and Stein 623 omit it.

9 Pelliot 764 recommences.

10 Pelliot 763, 764, 765 and Stein 623 " 'di". Pelliot 762 and 766 "de".

11 Stein 623 ends here.

12 Pelliot 763 and 765 have a shad here. Pelliot 766 has "la" here, and not a shad. Pelliot 762 and 764 have neither a shad nor "la".

13 Pelliot 762, 763, 764 and 765 "rnams su". Pelliot 766 abbreviates this to "rnamsu".

14 Pelliot 764, 765, and 766 "gcig la gcig". Pelliot 763 "gchig la gchig", with the "ga" of the second "gchig" below the line and the whole word rather sloppily squeezed in, in a different black ink. Pelliot 762 "gcig la gchig". It is noticeable that Pelliot 762's "gcig la gchig" is marked with a small light stroke above the first "ga" and after the last "ga" the tsheg is almost large enough to be a shad.

15 Pelliot 763, 765 and 766 "rten". Pelliot 762 "brten". Pelliot 764 "rten", or at least "brten" with the "ba" scratched a little, presumably to remove it.

16 Pelliot 762, 764, 765 and 766 "mdung khyim". Pelliot 763 "mdung kyim".

17 Pelliot 762, 763 and 765 "gyi". Pelliot 764 "gi". Pelliot 766 "dag gi".

18 Pelliot 763, 765, 764 and 766 "tshul". Pelliot 762 "tsul".

19 Pelliot 763, 765, 764 and 766 "gsum po". Pelliot 762 "gsuṃ po", with the anusvāra in the form of a relatively large circle.

20 Pelliot 764 is missing the following.

21 In Pelliot 766 the rest of this sentence has been torn away.

22 Pelliot 766 recommences.

ma lus par zhes bya [1]ba'i[2] tha tshig[3] go[4] //[5]

dris pa[6] / nyon mongs pa rnams[7] ni gang // las[8] dag[9] ni gang / sdug bsngal ni gang // rten pa'i[10] bye brag 'di dag gang [11] du ji[12] ltar[13] [14]bsdu bar[15] 'gyur[16] //

smras[17] pa[18] // « *dang po* [19] *brgyad dang* [20] *dgu nyon mongs //* »[21] bye brag bcu gnyis kyi[22] dang po ni ma rig pa'o[23] / brgyad pa ni sred pa[24] /

1 Pelliot 764 recommences.

2 Pelliot 762 and 766 "ma lus par zhes bya ba'i". Pelliot 763 "ma lus pa zhes bya ba'i". Pelliot 765 seems to have skipped a little with its "ma lus pa'i". (Pelliot 764 "ba'i".)

3 Pelliot 762, 764 and 765 "tha tshig". Pelliot 763 and 766 "tha tsig".

4 In Pelliot 764 there is a "gi gu" as well as a "na ro" above the "ga".

5 Pelliot 766 has black shad, red circle, black shad, red circle, black shad here.

6 Pelliot 762, 763, 765 and 766 "dris pa". Pelliot 764 "dris pa'".

7 Pelliot 762, 763, 765 and 766 have "rnams" here. Pelliot 764 omits it.

8 Pelliot 762, 763, 764 and 765 "las". Pelliot 766 "lag".

9 Pelliot 766 has "dag" here. Pelliot 762, 763, 764 and 765 omit it.

10 In Pelliot 763 something between "rten" and "pa'i" has been marked as an error and erased.

11 Pelliot 762, 764 and 766 add "dag" here. Pelliot 763 and 765 omit it.

12 Pelliot 762, 764 and 766 "ji". Pelliot 763 and 765 "ci".

13 Pelliot 765 ends here.

14 Stein 621.1 begins here. Throughout Stein 621.1 almost all black shads are doubled with a shadowing red shad, following or before.

15 Pelliot 763, 764, 766 and Stein 621.1 "bsdu bar". Pelliot 762 "bsdu' bar".

16 Pelliot 763, 764 and 766 " 'gyur". Pelliot 762 and Stein 621.1 " 'gyurd". In Pelliot 762 the " 'a chung" is inserted below the line.

17 Pelliot 764 ends here.

18 Pelliot 762, 763 and 766 "smras pa". Stein 621.1 "smras pa'". Use of " 'a chung" in positions like this is common in Tibetan texts from Dunhuang.

19 Pelliot 762 adds "dang" here. Pelliot 763, 766 and Stein 621.1 omit it.

20 Pelliot 762 has a double shad, two vertical circles and a double shad here. Pelliot 763, 766 and Stein 621.1 have no shads here.

21 Pelliot 762 does not use red ink for the quotations, but in Pelliot 762 vertical circles serve to mark some of the quotations.

22 Pelliot 766 and Stein 621.1 "bcu gnyis kyi". Pelliot 762 "bcu gnyis gi". Pelliot 763 "bcu gnyigs gyi".

23 Pelliot 762 and 766 "ma rig pa'o". Stein 621.1 "ma rig pa'". Pelliot 763 "ma rig pa".

24 Pelliot 763 and 766 "sred pa". Stein 621.1 "sred pa'". Pelliot 762 "sred pa'o".

dgu pa ni len pa ste / 'di[1] gsum ni nyon mongs pa[2] rnams su[3] shes par[4] bya'o[5] //

las de [6] gang zhe na[7] // « *gnyis*[8] *dang bcu pa las yin te* // »[9] gnyis pa ni 'du byed / bcu pa ni srid pa[10] ste / chos 'di[11] gnyis ni las su[12] bsdu bar[13] shes par bya'o //[14]

« *lhag ma bdun yang sdug bsngal yin* // »[15] nyon mongs pa dang las su[16] bsdus pa'i bye brag[17] de dag gi lhag ma[18] / bye brag bdun po gang yin ba[19] de dag ni / sdug bsngal du bsdu bar[20] shes par bya ste // 'di lta ste[21] rnam par[22] shes pa dang mying dang gzugs dang / skye mched[23] drug dang / reg pa dang / tshor ba dang /[24] skye ba dang / rga shi rnams so[25] // yang zhes bya ba'i sgra ni / bsdu ba ste // sdug pa dang bral ba [26] dang / myi

1 Pelliot 763 and Stein 621.1 " 'di". Pelliot 762 and 766 "de".
2 Pelliot 762, 763 and 766 "nyon mongs pa". Stein 621.1 "nyon mongs pa'".
3 Pelliot 762, 763 and Stein 621.1 "rnams su". Pelliot 766 abbreviates this to "rnamsu".
4 Pelliot 763, 766 and Stein 621.1 "shes par". Pelliot 762 "zhes par".
5 Pelliot 762, 763 and Stein 621.1 "bya'o". Pelliot 766 "bya' 'o".
6 Pelliot 763 adds "dag" here. Pelliot 762, 766 and Stein 621.1 omit it.
7 Pelliot 762, 763 and 766 "na". Stein 621.1 "na'".
8 Against the metre Stein 621.1 adds a "pa" here. Pelliot 762, 763 and 766 omit it.
9 Pelliot 762 does not use red ink for the quotations.
10 Pelliot 762, 763 and 766 "srid pa". Stein 621.1 "sred pa".
11 Pelliot 763 and Stein 621.1 " 'di". Pelliot 762 and 766 "de".
12 Pelliot 763 and Stein 621.1 "las su". Pelliot 762 and 766 abbreviate this to "lasu".
13 Stein 621.1 "bsdu bar". Pelliot 762 "bsdu' bar". Pelliot 766 "bsdus par". Pelliot 763 "bar".
14 Pelliot 762 has a double shad, two diagonal circles and a single shad here, surrounding a crossed out "lha".
15 Pelliot 762 does not use red ink for the quotations.
16 Pelliot 763, 766 and Stein 621.1 "las su". Pelliot 762 abbreviates this to "lasu".
17 Pelliot 762, 763 and 766 "bsdus pa'i bye brag". Stein 621.1 "bsdus pa".
18 Pelliot 762, 763 and Stein 621.1 "lhag ma". Pelliot 766 "lhag ma'".
19 Pelliot 762, 763, 766 and Stein 621.1 "yin ba", not "yin pa".
20 Pelliot 763, 766 and Stein 621.1 "bsdu bar". Pelliot 762 "bsdu' bar".
21 In Pelliot 766 " 'di lta ste" is added below the line.
22 Pelliot 762, 763 and 766 "rnam par". Stein 621.1 "rnams par".
23 Pelliot 762, 763 and 766 "skye mched". Stein 621.1 "skye mced".
24 Pelliot 763 ends here.
25 Pelliot 766 "rnams so". Pelliot 762 "rnamso". Stein 621.1 "rnams so'". In Stein 621.1 the extra " 'a chung" is below the "sa".
26 Pelliot 762 adds a "pa" here, which has not been crossed out or marked for deletion. Pelliot 766 and Stein 621.1 omit it.

sdug pa dang phrad pa dang / 'dod pas phongs pa'i[1] sdug bsngal rnams sdud do[2] //

[3]de'i phyir [4] chos bcu[5] gnyis po de[6] dag ni las dang nyon mongs pa[7] dang sdug bsngal rnams su 'dus par shes par bya'o // ni zhes bya ba'i[8] sgra ni lhag ma'i[9] tshig[10] bcad pa'i[11] don te // mdo las bstan pa'i chos rnams ni 'di dag du zad kyi[12] // de las gzhan ci[13] yang myed do zhes gcad pa'o //[14]

dris pa de dag ni 'tshal na[15] / nyon mongs pa dang / las dang / sdug bsngal 'di dag gang las gang 'byung ba [16] bstan du gsol[17] //

smras pa[18] « //[19] *gsum po*[20] *dag las gnyis 'byung ste*[21] // »[22] nyon mongs pa zhes bya ba gsum po[23] dag las / las zhes bya ba[24] gnyis 'byung [25]

1 Pelliot 766 and Stein 621.1 "phongs pa'i". Pelliot 762 " 'phongs pa'i".
2 Pelliot 766 and Stein 621.1 "sdud do". Pelliot 762 "bsdud do", but the "ba" has been marked for deletion.
3 Pelliot 762, 766 and Stein 621.1 omit the expected "« *bcu gnyis chos ni gsum du 'dus* // »".
4 Pelliot 762 adds "chos / " here. Pelliot 766 and Stein 621.1 omit it.
5 Pelliot 766 ends here.
6 Pelliot 762 "de". Stein 621.1 " 'di".
7 In Stein 621.1 an " 'a chung" has been erased between "nyon" and "mongs".
8 Pelliot 762 "bya ba'i". Stein 621.1 "bya ba ba'i".
9 Stein 621.1 "lhag ma'i". Pelliot 762 "lhag pa'i".
10 Stein 621.1 "tshig". Pelliot 762 "tshigs".
11 Stein 621.1 "bcad pa'i". Pelliot 762 "gchad pa'i".
12 Stein 621.1 "kyi". Pelliot 762 "gyi".
13 Stein 621.1 "ci". Pelliot 762 "ji".
14 Pelliot 762 "gchad pa'o //". Stein 621.1 "gca[d pa'o //]".
15 Pelliot 762 " 'tshal na". Stein 621.1 " 'tsal na' ".
16 Pelliot 762 adds "da" here, which has not been crossed out or marked for deletion. Stein 621.1 omits it.
17 Pelliot 762 "gsol". Stein 621.1 "gsold".
18 Pelliot 762 "smras pa". Stein 621.1 "smras pa' ".
19 Pelliot 762 has a single shad, two vertical circles and a single shad here. Stein 621.1 has a double shad.
20 Stein 621.1 "« *gsum po* »". Pelliot 762 "*gsuṃ po*", with the anusvāra in the form of a relatively large circle.
21 Stein 621.1 "« *'byung ste* »". Pelliot 762 " *'byungs te*".
22 Pelliot 762 does not use red ink for the quotations.
23 Stein 621.1 "gsum po". Pelliot 762 "gsuṃ po", with the anusvāra in the form of a relatively large circle.
24 Pelliot 762 "zhes bya ba". Stein 621.1 "shes bya ba".
25 In Stein 621.1 a letter has been erased here.

ngo « //[1] *gnyis las bdun 'byung*[2] //[3] »[4] sdug bsngal[5] zhes bya ba gong du bstan pa rnams so[6] //[7] « *bdun las kyang*[8] *gsum*[9] *'byung* //[10] »[11] nyon mongs pa zhes bya ba rnams so[12] // yang nyon mongs pa zhes bya ba[13] gsum po[14] de[15] dag las / gnyis 'byung ste //[16] « *srid pa'i*[17] *'khor lo de // nyid ni yang dang yang du 'khor*d //[18] »[19] srid pa ni gsum ste / 'dod pa dang / gzugs [20]dang / gzugs[21] myed pa zhes bya ste[22] / de dag du myi

1 Pelliot 762 has a single shad, two vertical circles and a single shad here. Stein 621.1 has a double shad.

2 In Pelliot 762 the " 'a chung" of " '*byung*" is below the line.

3 Pelliot 762 has a single shad, two vertical circles and a single shad here. Stein 621.1 has a double shad.

4 Pelliot 762 does not use red ink for the quotations.

5 In Stein 621.1 something has been erased between "sdug" and "bsngal". It looks as if "bsngal" was begun, ran into the circle marking the position of the hole, was erased and rewritten to the right of the circle.

6 Stein 621.1 "rnams so'". In Stein 621.1 the " 'a chung" is below the "sa". Pelliot 762 "rnamso".

7 Pelliot 762 has a single shad, two vertical circles and a single shad here. Stein 621.1 has a double shad.

8 Stein 621.1 "« *kyang* »". Pelliot 762 "*gyang*".

9 Stein 621.1 "« *gsum* »". Pelliot 762 "*gsuṃ*", with the anusvāra in the form of a relatively large circle.

10 Pelliot 762 has a single shad, two vertical circles and a single shad here. Stein 621.1 has a double shad.

11 Pelliot 762 does not use red ink for the quotations.

12 Stein 621.1 "rnams so'". In Stein 621.1 the " 'a chung" is below the "sa". Pelliot 762 "rnamso".

13 Pelliot 762 "zhes bya ba". Stein 621.1 omits it.

14 Stein 621.1 "gsum po". Pelliot 762 "gsuṃ po", with the anusvāra in the form of a relatively large circle.

15 Stein 621.1 has "de" here. Pelliot 762 omits it.

16 Pelliot 762 has a single shad, two vertical circles and a single shad here. Stein 621.1 has a double shad.

17 Stein 621.1 "« *srid pa' i* »". Pelliot 762 "*srid par*".

18 Pelliot 762 has a double shad, two vertical circles and a single shad here. Stein 621.1 has a double shad.

19 Pelliot 762 does not use red ink for the quotations.

20 Stein 620 begins here.

21 Pelliot 762 and Stein 620 "gzugs". Stein 621.1 "gzus".

22 Stein 621.1 "bya ste". Pelliot 762 and Stein 620 "bya ba ste".

sdod par 'khor ba'i[1] 'khor lor[2] [3]gyur pa /[4] so so'i skye bo'i 'jig rten 'di[5] bdag nyid kun du 'phyan[6] to // ni zhes bya ba'i sgra ni / nges pa myed par[7] bstan pa'i don te[8] // ji ltar 'khor lo rims[9] gyis[10] 'khor ba[11] de ltar / srid pa rnams su[12] 'byung ba ma[13].yin gyi[14] nges pa[15] myed par bstan to //

dris pa //[16] 'o na lus thams cad kyi[17] dbang phyug sems can[18] zhes bgyi ba[19] de gang lags // de'i bgyid pa[20] [21] ji lta bu[22] //

1 Stein 620 and 621.1 " 'khor ba'i". Pelliot 762 " 'khord ba'i".
2 Stein 620 and 621.1 " 'khor lor". Pelliot 762 " 'khor lo /".
3 Stein 621.1 continues as Ch.73.VII.9 here.
4 Pelliot 762 "gyur". Stein 620 "gyurd pa /". Stein 621.1 "gyur pa //".
5 Pelliot 762 and Stein 620 " 'di". Stein 621.1 " 'dir".
6 Stein 620 and 621.1 " 'phyan". Pelliot 762 "phyin".
7 Pelliot 762 and Stein 620 "myed par". Stein 621.1 looks more like "myed pa' ra", perhaps the beginning of "myed pa'i" changed to "par".
8 In Pelliot 762 this looks like "de". In Stein 620 and 621.1 it is clearly "te".
9 In Stein 620 the "sa" of "rims" is below the line. Finding a letter which is expected to follow another letter but appears below it instead is common in Tibetan texts from Dunhuang.
10 Stein 620 and 621.1 "gyis". Pelliot 762 "gis".
11 Stein 620 and 621.1 have " 'khor ba" here. Pelliot 762 omits it.
12 Stein 620 and 621.1 "rnams su". Pelliot 762 abbreviates this to "rnamsu".
13 In Stein 621.1 a cross marks the insertion of "ma" which looks like a later correction in another hand.
14 Pelliot 762 "yin gyi". Stein 621.1 "yin gyi", with an erased letter, perhaps "pa", between "yin" and "gyi". Stein 620 "yin kyi".
15 Pelliot 762 and Stein 620 "nges pa". Stein 621.1 "nges pa'".
16 Pelliot 762 "dris pa //". Stein 620 "dris pa". Stein 621.1 "dris pa' //".
17 Stein 620 and 621.1 "thams cad kyi". Pelliot 762 "thams chad gyi".
18 Stein 620 and 621.1 "sems can". Pelliot 762 "sems chan".
19 Stein 620 and 621.1 "bgyi ba". Pelliot 762 "bya ba".
20 Stein 620 and 621.1 "bgyid pa". Pelliot 762 "byed pa".
21 Stein 620 and 621.1 add "ni" here. Pelliot 762 omits it.
22 Pelliot 762 and Stein 620 "ji lta bu". Stein 621.1 "ci ltar bu", though the "ra" is partially erased.

smras pa[1] /[2] « *'gro kun*[3] *rgyu dang 'bras bu ste //*[4] »[5] btags pa[6] ma gtogs par « /[7] *'di la*[8] *sems can*[9] *gzhan ci'ang*[10] *myed //*[11] »[12] [13] 'di ni yang dag pa brtags pa[14] ste / btags pa tsam[15] ni ma yin no // btags pa tsam gyi[16] tshul du[17] yod pa de ni rdzas su yod par myi rung ngo //

dris pa /[18] gal te de ltar na[19] / 'o na 'jig rten 'di nas 'jig rten[20] pha rol du su mchi[21] //

1 Pelliot 762 and Stein 620 "smras pa". Stein 621.1 "smras pa'", with the " 'a chung" placed below the "pa".
2 Pelliot 762 has a single shad, one circle and a single shad here. Stein 620 and 621.1 have a double shad.
3 In Pelliot 762 something has been written between " *'gro*" and "*kun*", but has been crossed out.
4 Pelliot 762 has a single shad, two vertical circles and a single shad here. Stein 620 and 621.1 have a double shad.
5 Text found between these chevrons or guillemets français appears in red ink in Stein 620 and 621.1, though the final shad in Stein 620 is in black here. Pelliot 762 does not use red ink for the quotations.
6 Pelliot 762 and Stein 620 "btags pa". Stein 621.1 "btags pa'".
7 Pelliot 762 has a single shad, one circle and a single shad here. Stein 621.1 has a double shad. Stein 620 has a single shad.
8 Stein 620 "« *'di la* »". Pelliot 762 " *'di la*". Stein 621.1 "« *'di las* »".
9 Stein 620 and 621.1 "« *sems can* »". Pelliot 762 "*sems chan*".
10 Stein 620 "« *ji'ang* »". Pelliot 762 "*ji yang*", against the metre. Stein 621.1 "« *ci yang* »", against the metre.
11 Pelliot 762 has a single shad, one circle and a single shad here. Stein 620 and 621.1 have a double shad.
12 Pelliot 762 does not use red ink for the quotations.
13 In Stein 620 there is interlinear text below this next phrase.
14 Pelliot 762 and Stein 620 "brtags pa". Stein 621.1 "brtaggs ba".
15 Stein 620 and 621.1 "tsam". Pelliot 762 "tsham".
16 Stein 621.1 "tsam gyi". Stein 620 "tsam kyi". Pelliot 762 "tsham gyi".
17 Stein 620 and 621.1 "tshul du". Pelliot 762 "yul du".
18 Pelliot 762 "dris pa /", though the shad is very sloppy and high. Stein 620 "dris pa". Stein 621.1 "dris pa' /".
19 Stein 621.1 "de ltar na". Pelliot 762 and Stein 620 "de lta na".
20 In Pelliot 762 something has been crossed out between " 'jig" and "rten", perhaps a poorly formed "rte".
21 Stein 620 "mchi". Stein 621.1 "mchi' ". Pelliot 762 "mci' ".

smras pa[1] // [2] 'di nas 'jig rten pha rol[3] du rdul phra mo[4] tsam[5] yang myi 'pho ste[6] / 'on kyang // « *stong[7] pa kho na'i chos rnams las // stong pa'i chos rnams 'byung bar zad //* »[8] bdag dang bdag gi myed pa'i chos nyon mongs pa dang las[9] rgyur gyur pa[10] lnga po stong pa[11] rnams las bdag dang bdag gi[12] myed pa / sdug bsngal du brjod pa' / 'bras bur btags pa'i chos stong pa[13] bdun po dag 'byung bar 'gyur ro zhes bya ba'i[14] tha tshig[15] go // de ni 'di skad du [16]bdag dang bdag gi[17] myed la / de[18] phan tshun du yang bdag gi ma yin te / 'on kyang rang bzhin[19] gyis[20] bdag myed pa'i chos rnams[21] las // rang bzhin gyis[22] bdag myed pa'i chos

1 Pelliot 762 and Stein 620 "smras pa". Stein 621.1 "smras pa'".

2 Pelliot 762 adds " 'jig rten" here. Stein 620 and 621.1 omit it.

3 In Stein 620 the paper has a hole in it, possibly from overly vigorous erasing, but "rol" is the obvious reading.

4 Pelliot 762 and Stein 620 "pha rol du dngos po rdul phra mo". Stein 621.1 "pha rol du dngos po rdul".

5 Stein 620 and 621.1 "tsam". Pelliot 762 "tsham".

6 Stein 620 and 621.1 " 'pho ste". Pelliot 762 " 'pho' ste".

7 In Pelliot 762 a "na" has been crossed out between the "*sto*" and "*nga*" of "*stong*", suggesting "*sto*n" was written in error for "*stong*" but was immediately noticed and corrected.

8 Pelliot 762 does not use red ink for this quotation, neither does it use its usual vertical dots.

Pelliot 762 ends here, on the second line of its fifth panel. There was ample room to have continued so this must be an unfinished manuscript (as opposed to the survival of a manuscript now missing its last parts but once complete).

9 Stein 620 "las". Stein 621.1 "las dang /".

10 Stein 620 "gyurd pa". Stein 621.1 "gyur pa'i".

11 Stein 620 "stong pa". Stein 621.1 "stongs pa".

12 Stein 620 "gi". Stein 621.1 "gyi".

13 Stein 620 "stong pa". Stein 621.1 "stong".

14 Stein 620 "bya ba'i". Stein 621.1 "bya ba".

15 Stein 620 "tha tshig". Stein 621.1 "tha tsig".

16 In Stein 621.1 a letter has been crossed out in black and red, perhaps the beginning of a "ga".

17 Stein 621.1 "bdag gi". Stein 620 "bdag".

18 Stein 620 "de". Stein 621.1 "de dag".

19 In Stein 621.1 the "zha" and "na" of "bzhin" are written over the top of the circle marking the place for a string hole.

20 Stein 621.1 "gyis". Stein 620 "kyis".

21 Stein 621.1 "rnams". Stein 620 "rnams rnams".

22 Stein 621.1 "gyis". Stein 620 "kyis".

rnams 'byung bar / de ltar khong du chud par[1] bya'o zhes[2] bstan pa[3] yin no //

'dir dris [4]pa[5] / rang bzhin gyis[6] bdag ma mchis pa'i[7] chos kho na dag las // rang bzhin gyis[8] bdag ma mchis pa'i[9] chos kho na dag 'byung ba 'di la dpe ji mchis[10] //

'dir smras pa[11] // « *kha ton mar mye mye long rgya*[12] // *mye shel sa bon skyur dang sgras* // » dpe 'di rnams dang btags pas kyang rang bzhin gyis[13] bdag myed pa dang / 'jig rten pha rol du phyin pa[14] 'grub par shes [15]par bya'o //

dper na bla ma'i kha nas[16] brjod pa rnams slob ma la 'pho na ni / bla mas brjod du myed par 'gyurd bas[17] myi 'pho'o // slob mas[18] smra ba yang gzhan las ma yin te / rgyu myed par 'gyur ba'i[19] phyir ro // ji ltar bla ma'i[20] kha nas brjod pa ltar 'chi ka'i sems kyang de bzhin te / rtag pa'i skyon du 'gyur bas[21] 'jig rten[22] pha rol du [23] myi[24] 'gro'o // 'jig rten pha

1 Stein 620 "chud par". Stein 621.1 "chung bar".
2 In Stein 621.1, before "zhes", a "sa" has been begun.
3 Stein 620 "bstan pa". Stein 621.1 "bstan pa'".
4 In Stein 620 [upper left corner of 69b] there once appeared one of the "Ch." numbers in red ink, but it has been scribbled out in black ink and is illegible.
5 Stein 620 "dris pa". Stein 621.1 "dris pa'".
6 Stein 621.1 "gyis". Stein 620 "kyis".
7 Stein 620 "mchis pa'i". Stein 621.1 "mcis pa'i".
8 Stein 621.1 "gyis". Stein 620 "kyis".
9 Stein 620 "ma mchis pa'i". Stein 621.1 "maṃcis pa'i".
10 Stein 620 "ji mchis". Stein 621.1 "chi mcis".
11 Stein 620 "smras pa". Stein 621.1 "smras pa'".
12 Stein 620 "*rgya*". Stein 621.1 "*rgya'*".
13 Stein 621.1 "gyis". Stein 620 "kyis".
14 Stein 621.1 omits "du phyin pa". Stein 620 has it.
15 In Stein 620 a "ra" has been crossed out.
16 Stein 620 "kha nas". Stein 621.1 "khams nas".
17 Stein 620 "myed par 'gyurd bas". Stein 621.1 "myed pas", suggesting an inadvertent skip.
18 Stein 621.1 "slob mas". Stein 620 "slob ma".
19 Stein 620 " 'gyur ba'i". Stein 621.1 " 'gyurd ba'i".
20 Stein 620 "bla ma'i". Stein 621.1 "bla ma".
21 Stein 620 " 'gyur ba'i". Stein 621.1 " 'gyurd bas".
22 In Stein 621.1 before "rten" a letter was begun, perhaps "ya".
23 Stein 621.1 adds "yang". Stein 620 omits it.
24 In Stein 621.1 a letter has been erased before "myi".

rol yang gzhan[1] las myi 'byung ste / rgyu myed pa'i skyon du 'gyur ro // ji ltar[2] bla mas[3] brjod pa'i rgyu las 'byung ba[4] / slob ma'i de nyid / de dang gzhan no zhes brjod par myi [5]nus pa ltar 'chi ka'i[6] sems la brten nas skye ba'i char gtogs pa'i sems kyang de bzhin te // de dag de nyid dang / de las gzhan zhes brjod par myi nus so[7] //

de bzhin du ji ltar mar mye las mar mye[8] dang / bzhin las mye long du / gzugs brnyan 'byung ba dang / rgya las rgya'i 'bur[9] dang / mye shel las mye dang / sa bon las[10] myu gu dang / shing tog skyur po'i sgyus[11] 'gram chu[12] ldang ba dang / sgra las brag ca[13] 'byung bar 'gyur zhing / de dag [14] kyang de nyid dang / gzhan zhes shes par sla ba ma yin ba[15] de bzhin[16] du //

« *phung po*[17] *nying mtshams sbyor ba dang // myi*[18] *'pho bar yang mkhas rtogs bya*[19] *//* »[20] de la phung po ni gzugs dang / tshor ba dang / 'du shes dang / 'du byed[21] dang[22] / [23]rnam par shes pa'i phung po'o // de dag

1 In Stein 621.1 "gzhan" is preceded by a poorly formed " 'a chung".
2 Stein 621.1 "ji ltar". Stein 620 "ci ltar".
3 Stein 620 "bla mas". Stein 621.1 "bla ma".
4 Stein 621.1 " 'byung ba". Stein 620 "byung ba".
5 In Stein 620 the hole in the paper comes through here.
6 Stein 620 " 'chi ka'i". Stein 621.1 " 'chi kha'i".
7 Stein 620 "so". Stein 621.1 "so'" with the " 'a chung" below the "sa".
8 Stein 621.1 "mar mye". Stein 620 "mye".
9 Stein 621.1 "rgya'i 'bur". Stein 620 " 'bur".
10 Stein 620 "las". Stein 621.1 "las las".
11 Stein 620 "shing tog skyur po'i sgyus". Stein 621.1 "shing tog skyur po'i rgyus".
12 Stein 621.1 " 'gram chu". Stein 620 " 'gram cu".
13 Stein 620 "brag ca". Stein 621.1 "brag ca'".
14 Stein 620 has "las" here but it is marked for deletion with two ticks. Stein 621.1 omits it.
15 Stein 620 and 621.1 "yin ba", not "yin pa".
16 In Stein 621.1 something has been erased from between the "ba" and the "zha" in "bzhin", an erroneous "de" perhaps.
17 Stein 620 "*phung po*". Stein 621.1 "« *phung po*'i »".
18 In Stein 621.1 it is interesting to note that a standard "ma" is written in red and the "ya btags" and "gi gu" are added in black.
19 Stein 620 "*rtogs bya*". Stein 621.1 "« *rtog bya*' »".
20 Strikingly Stein 620 does not use the expected red ink here. Stein 621.1 does.
21 Stein 620 " 'du byed". Stein 621.1 " 'du' byed".
22 Stein 620 "dang". Stein 621.1 "deng".
Stein 620 ends here.
23 Pelliot 768 begins here.

gi[1] [2] nying mtshams[3] sbyor ba ni / 'gags nas rgyu de las 'byung ba' // gzhan dag 'byung ba ste // 'jig rten 'di nas[4] 'jig rten pha rol du dngos po [5]rdul phra mo[6] tsam 'ga'[7] yang myi 'gro'o // de ltar na / 'khor ba'i 'khor lo / nor ba'i[8] rnam par rtog pa'i bag chags kyis bskyed pa yin no //

tha ma'i[9] yang zhes[10] bya ba'i sgra ni ldog pa[11] ste // de [12]las bzlog par[13] shes par bya'o[14] // dngos po rnams la / myi rtag pa dang / sdug bsngal ba [15]dang / stong pa dang / bdag myed par brtags na[16] / dngos po[17] la rmongs par myi 'gyur[18] ro // rmongs pa myed na myi chags so[19] // ma chags[20] na zhe sdang bar mi 'gyur[21] ro // zhe sdang myed na las myi byed[22] [23]do // las myed na dngos po myi len to // len pa [24]myed na srid pa mngon bar 'du myi byed do // srid pa myed na myi skye'o // ma skyes na [25] sems la[26] sdug bsngal myi 'byung ngo // de ltar 'dir rgyu lnga po de ma

1 Stein 621.1 "de dag gi". Pelliot 768 has "de dgi", either by way of abbreviation or as the result of too much haste.
2 Pelliot 768 adds "nyid" here. Stein 621.1 omits it.
3 Pelliot 768 "mtshams". Stein 621.1 "mtsams".
4 Pelliot 768 omits " 'jig rten 'di nas" here. Stein 621.1 has it.
5 Stein 624 begins here. In Stein 624 some black shads are doubled with a shadowing red shad following.
6 Pelliot 768 and Stein 621.1 have "phra mo". Stein 624 omits it.
7 Pelliot 768 and Stein 621.1 " 'ga' ". In Stein 624 there is something after "tsam" which includes "ga" but it is illegible.
8 Stein 621.1 and 624 "nor ba'i". Pelliot 768 "nor pa'i".
9 Stein 621.1 "tha ma'i". Stein 624 "tha ma". Pelliot 768 "mtha ma'i".
10 Pelliot 768 and Stein 624 "zhes". Stein 621.1 "shes".
11 In Stein 621.1 "pa" has been inserted into the text, marked by an x.
12 The next few words in Stein 624 are illegible.
13 Stein 621.1 "bzlog par". Pelliot 768 "bzlog pa'i". Stein 624 is illegible.
14 Pelliot 768 "shes par bya'o". Stein 621.1 "shers par bya' 'o". Stein 624 is illegible.
15 Stein 624 is more legible for the next few words.
16 Pelliot 768 and Stein 624 "na". Stein 621.1 "na' ".
17 Pelliot 768 and Stein 624 "dngos po". Stein 621.1 "dngos".
18 Pelliot 768 and Stein 624 " 'gyur". Stein 621.1 " 'gyurd".
19 Pelliot 768 "chags so". Stein 621.1 and 624 "chags so' ".
20 Pelliot 768 and Stein 624 "chags". Stein 621.1 "cags".
21 Pelliot 768 " 'gyur". Stein 621.1 and 624 " 'gyurd".
22 Pelliot 768 and Stein 621.1 "myi byed". Stein 624 "myed".
23 The next few words in Stein 624 are illegible.
24 Stein 624 is more legible for the next few words.
25 Stein 624 adds "ni". Pelliot 768 and Stein 621.1 omit it.
26 Pelliot 768, Stein 621.1 and 624 all have "sems la", rather than "lus dang sems la".

bstsags pas // gzhan du 'bras [1]bu myi 'byung ste / 'di ni[2] thar pa zhes bya'o // [3]de ltar na[4] rtag pa[5] dang / chad pa'i[6] mtha' la stsogs pa lta ba ngan pa[7] rnams bsald pa[8] yin no //

'di la tshigs su[9] bcad pa gnyis yod de //

« shin du phra ba'i dngos la yang //
gang gis [10]chad par[11] rnam brtags pa[12] //
rnam par [13]myi mkhas de yis[14] ni //
rkyen las 'byung ba'i[15] don ma mthong //

'di las bstsal ba *gang yang myed //*[16]
gzhag par bya ba ci[17] yang myed //
yang dag nyid la yang dag blta[18] //
yang dag mthong [19]na rnam par grol[20] // »[21]

1 The next few words in Stein 624 are illegible.
2 Pelliot 768 " 'di ni". Stein 621.1 " 'di". Stein 624 is illegible.
3 Stein 624 is more legible for the next few words.
4 Pelliot 768 and Stein 621.1 "na". 624 "na'".
5 Pelliot 768 and Stein 621.1 "rtag pa". Stein 624 "rtag pa'".
6 Pelliot 768 and Stein 624 "chad pa'i". Stein 621.1 "cad pa'i".
7 Pelliot 768 "ngan pa". Stein 624 "ngan pa' /". Stein 621.1 "ngan pa", but preceded by a half erased word beginning with "da" or something similar, and formerly written as "ngan par" with the "ra" now mostly erased.
8 Stein 621.1 "bsald pa". Pelliot 768 and Stein 624 "bstsald pa".
9 Stein 621.1 "tsigs su". Stein 624 has the abbreviated "tshigsu". Pelliot 768 "tshigs".
10 The next few words in Stein 624 are illegible.
11 Pelliot 768 "*chad par*". Stein 621.1 "« *cad par* »". Stein 624 is illegible.
12 Pelliot 768 "*pa*". Stein 621.1 "« *pa'* »". Stein 624 is illegible.
13 Stein 624 is more legible for the next few words.
14 Stein 621.1 and 624 "« *de yis* »". Pelliot 768 "*de ' is*".
15 Stein 621.1 "« 'byung ba'i »". Stein 624 "« byung ba'i »". Pelliot 768 "byung ba'i". None of the manuscripts has "« *skyes pa' i* »".
16 Pelliot 768 " *'di las bstsal ba gang yang myed //*". Stein 624 "« *'di las bstsal* ba *gang yang myed //* »", and there appears to be one further letter after "« *myed* »" but it is illegible, perhaps it is "da" or "ra". Stein 621.1 "« *'di las* ba' *bstsal bya gang myed //* »".
17 Stein 621.1 and 624 "« *ci* »". Pelliot 768 "*ji*".
18 Pelliot 768 "*blta*". Stein 621.1 and 624 "« *lta'* »".
19 The next few words in Stein 624 are illegible.
20 Pelliot 768 "*grol*". Stein 621.1 "« *grold* »". Stein 624 is illegible.
21 Pelliot 768 does not use red ink for the quotation.

[1]rten cing 'brel par[2] 'byung ba'i snying po rnam par bshad pa' /[3] slob dpon[4] klu sgrub kyis[5] mdzad pa [6]rdzogs so[7] // //[8]

1 Stein 624 is more legible for the next few words.

2 Stein 621.1 and 624 " 'brel par". Pelliot 768 " 'brel pa'r", though the second " 'a chung" is almost erased.

3 Stein 621.1 marks this title with fancy patterns among the shads at each end of it.

4 Stein 621.1 "slob dpon". Pelliot 768 and Stein 624 "slobs dpon".

5 Pelliot 768 and Stein 624 "kyis". Stein 621.1 "gyis".

6 The next few words in Stein 624 are illegible.

7 Pelliot 768 "rdzogs so". Stein 621.1 abbreviates this to "rdzogs'o", with the " 'a chung" below the "sa".

8 Pelliot 768, Stein 621.1 and 624 end here, though 624 continues with "// / // dad pa'i thugs" and then a line in larger letters "tad dya tha sa ḍa / nad ṭe / na nad ṭe / 'a na do / nad ḍi kund daṃ sba' ha' //".

Clarification of an Interpretation of the Heart of Dependent Origination[1]

(taken from Dunhuang manuscripts)

[rgya gar skad du /

pra ti' tya sa mud pa' da hri da ya
bya khya na' bhi sma ra ṇa //

bod skad du //

rten cing 'brel par 'byung ba'i snying po'i
rnam par bshad pa'i brjed byang //]

1 Stein 621.2 (Tibetan MSS Tun Huang Collection Volume 4, the second part of original number Ch.73.VII.9, Catalogue number 621.2, Folios 74a-80a, [the second part of MS 596]) and Stein 622 (Tibetan MSS Tun Huang Collection Volume 34, Original number Ch.51.I.23 [42], Catalogue number 622, Folios 53a-56b, [MS 597]) are edited here.

[1]rten cing 'brel par 'byung ba 'di la[2] //

dge sbyong / nyan 'dod pa / mnyan pa dang /[3] gzung ba[4] dang / khong du chud par[5] bya ba dang / rtog pa dang / sel nus pa dang / ldan ba'i[6] slob ma zhig / slob dpon[7] gyi gan du 'ongs nas // de bzhin gshegs pa'i bstan pa las[8] brtsams ste / 'di skad 'dri'o[9] // bcom ldan[10] 'das 'di la //[11] *rten cing 'brel par 'byung ba'i yan lag gi*[12] *bye brag bcu gnyis thub pas gsungs pa*[13] //[14] de dag gang du bsdu bar[15] blta ba thos par 'dod do //

de chos de dag gi de kho na nyid 'dri bar rig nas // slobs dpon gyis[16] 'di skad ces bu // *de dag*[17] *ni nyon mongs pa dang / las dang / sdug bsngal*

1 Stein 621.2 and 622 begin here. Stein 621.2 often has reversed "gi gu", Stein 622 has none. Stein 621.2 and Stein 622 often have " 'a chung" with a flag.

2 Stein 622 "la". Stein 621.2 "la'".

3 Stein 622 "dge sbyong / nyan 'dod pa / mnyan pa dang /". Stein 621.2 "dge sbyong nyan 'dod pas bnyan pa dang //".

4 Stein 622 "gzung ba". Stein 621.2 "bzung ba".

5 Stein 622 "chud par". Stein 621.2 "cud par".

6 Stein 621.2 and 622 have "ldan ba'i", not "ldan pa'i".

7 Stein 622 "slob dpon". Stein 621.2 "slobs dpon".

8 Stein 621.2 "las". Stein 622 "la".

9 Stein 622 " 'dri'o". Stein 621.2 has " 'dri 'a'o", i.e. " 'dri" then " 'a chung" + " 'a chung" with "na ro").

10 In Stein 621.2 it would appear that "bco" was written followed by the commencement of the "la" of "ldan", then the final "ma" of "bcom" was remembered, and finally "ldan" was written in its proper place.

11 In Stein 622 this double shad is in fact: a shad, followed by two vertical circles, and a shad. (Here and below these are quite different from both ordinary shads and the familiar "tsheg shad" or "dotted shads". Their purpose appears to be as markers, often for quotations. They appear in both Stein 621.2 and Stein 622 but more often in the latter than in the former.)

12 Stein 622 "gi". Stein 621.2 omits it.

13 Stein 622 "gsungs pa". Stein 621.2 has "gsungs pa'" with the " 'a chung" below the line.

14 In Stein 622 this double shad is in fact: a shad, followed by two vertical circles, and a shad.

15 Stein 622 "gang du bsdu bar". Stein 621.2 has "gang sdu bar" and something has been erased between the "sdu" and "bar", possibly "sdug bsngal bar" had been written erroneously for "sdu bar".

16 Stein 621.2 "slobs dpon gyis". Stein 622 "slobs dpon gis".

17 In Stein 621.2 "dag" was preceded by a "ba" or a small " 'a chung" which has been erased.

rnams su 'dus te[1] */ gsum po 'di dag du ji lta ba*[2] *bzhin no //*

zhes gsal zhing zur phyin pa'i tshig[3] 'di skad smras so[4] // de la gnyis dang bcu ni bcu[5] gnyis so[6] // yan lag rnams nyid bye brag pas na // yan lag[7] gi bye brag ste / shing rta'i [8] yan lag bzhin du yan lag du gyur pa bstan to[9] // lus dang ngag[10] thub pas na thub pa'o // thub pa des gsungs pa zhes bya ba ni //[11] bstan pa dang bshad pa zhes bya ba'i rnam grangs su gtogs pa'o // de yang rang bzhin dang / nges pa dang / skye bu[12] dang / gzhan la rag las pa dang / dbang phyug dang / dus dang / ngo bo nyid dang / kha rje dang / stes dbang dang / gyi na la stsogs pa'i rgyu rnams la stsogs pa[13] ni ma yin te // de ni rten cing 'brel par 'byung ba'o // yan lag bcu gnyis kyi bye brag ni[14] de dag ni / nyon mongs pa dang / las dang / sdug bsngal[15] rnams su gcig la gcig brten te / shing gsum rtse sprad pa'i tshul[16] ji lta[17] ba bzhin / gsum po dag du 'du bar[18] 'gyur ro // ji lta ba bzhin zhes bya ba ni / ma lus par[19] zhes bya ba'i tha tsig go[20] //

1 Stein 622 "te". Stein 621.2 "ste".
2 Stein 622 "ji lta ba". Stein 621.2 "ji lta".
3 Stein 622 "tshig". Stein 621.2 "tsig".
4 In Stein 621.2 "so" includes an " 'a chung" below its "sa". Sentence final "o" is followed by an " 'a chung" elsewhere in the text, sometimes below it, sometimes following to the right.
5 In Stein 622 an erroneous "gi gu" has been erased here.
6 Stein 622 "so". Stein 621.2 "so'".
7 In Stein 621.2 "lag" appears to be preceded by some letter or mark. It looks as if a "ya" was begun, the error noticed, and "lag" was written next.
8 In Stein 622 "pha" has been crossed out.
9 Stein 622 "to". Stein 621.2 "to'".
10 In Stein 622 an extra "ga" clearly preceding "ngag" would make the manuscript reading odd except that there is a mark suggesting it is meant to be crossed out. Here "ngag" parallels "gsung" just as "lus" does "sku" and Stein 621.2 and 622 both omit the expected "thugs" or its parallel in this phrase.
11 In Stein 622 this double shad is in fact: a shad, followed by a design of three circles, and a shad.
12 Stein 622 "skye bu". Stein 621.2 "skyes bu".
13 Stein 621.2 "la stsogs pa". Stein 622 "las stsogs pa".
14 Stein 622 "ni". Stein 621.2 omits it.
15 Stein 622 "sdug bsngal". Stein 621.2 "bsdug bsngal".
16 Stein 622 "tshul". Stein 621.2 "tsul".
17 Stein 621.2 "ji lta". In Stein 622 "ji lta" is a replacement for something erased.
18 Stein 622 " 'du bar". Stein 621.2 " 'du' bar".
19 Stein 621.2 "ma lus par". Stein 622 "ma lus pa".
20 Stein 622 "tha tsig go". Stein 621.2 "tha tsigs so'" with the " 'a chung" below the "sa".

dris pa /[1] nyon mongs pa[2] rnams[3] ni gang / las ni gang / sdug bsngal ni gang / rten pa'i[4] bye brag 'di dag[5] / gang dag du ji ltar bsdu bar 'gyur[6] //

smras pa //[7] *dang po dang / brgyad pa dang / dgu pa ni nyon mongs pa yin no* //[8] bye brag bcu gnyis po de[9] dag gi dang po ni ma rig pa[10] / brgyad pa ni sred pa / dgu pa ni len pa[11] ste // de dag gsum ni nyon mongs pa[12] rnams su shes par bya'o //

las de dag gang zhe na *gnyis pa dang / bcu pa*'o[13] //[14] gnyis pa ni 'du byed / bcu pa ni sred pa[15] ste // 'di gnyis ni[16] las su bsdu bar shes par bya'o[17] //[18]

lhag ma bdun yang sdug bsngal yin te //[19] nyon mongs pa dang / las su bsdu ba'i bye brag[20] de dag gi[21] lhag ma[22] / bye brag bdun po gang

1 Stein 622 "dris pa /". Stein 621.2 "dris pa'".

2 In Stein 622 "nyon nyo mangs pa" found in the manuscript is in error for "nyon mongs pa".

3 Stein 622 "rnams". Stein 621.2 omits it.

4 Stein 621.2 "rten pa'i". Stein 622 "brten pa'i".

5 In Stein 621.2 " 'di dag" is added below the line.

6 Stein 622 " 'gyur". Stein 621.2 " 'gyurd".

7 Stein 621.2 has "da /" where this double shad is expected.

8 In Stein 622 this double shad is in fact: a shad, followed by two vertical circles, and a shad.

9 Following Stein 622. Stein 621.2 has " 'po" here and omits the "de".

10 Stein 622 "ma rig pa". Stein 621.2 "ma rig pa'".

11 Following Stein 622. Stein 621.2 has "len pa'" here, the " 'a chung" is below the "pa" and something has been erased between the "len" and the "pa'".

12 Stein 622 "nyon mongs pa". Stein 621.2 "nyon mongs pa'".

13 Stein 622 "bcu pa'o". Stein 621.2 "bcu' pa' 'o".

14 In Stein 622 this double shad is in fact: a shad, followed by two vertical circles, and a shad.

15 Stein 621.2 and 622 "sred pa". Here "srid pa" would be expected.

16 Stein 622 "ni". Stein 621.2 omits it.

17 Stein 622 "bya'o". Stein 621.2 has "bya 'a'o", i.e. "bya" then " 'a chung" + " 'a chung" with "na ro".

18 In Stein 622 this double shad is in fact: a shad, followed by two vertical circles, and a shad.

19 In Stein 622 this double shad is in fact: a shad, followed by two vertical circles, and a shad.

20 Stein 621.2 "byed brag". Stein 622 has "brag" where "bye brag" would be expected.

21 Stein 622 "de dag gi". Stein 621.2 has "de", below the line, followed by the abbreviation "dgi" which combines to signify "de dag gi".

22 Stein 622 "lhag ma". Stein 621.2 "lhag ma'".

yin ba[1] / de dag ni sdug bsngal du[2] bsdu bar shes par bya[3] ste // rnam par[4] shes pa dang / mying dang gzugs dang / skye mched[5] drug dang / reg pa dang / tshor ba dang / skye ba dang / rga shi rnams so[6] //[7] yang zhes bya ba'i sgras bsdu ba ste[8] // sdug pa[9] dang bral ba dang / myi sdug pa dang phrad pa dang / 'dod pa myi rnyed pa'i sdug bsngal rnams su[10] bsdu bar bya'o //[11]

[12]chos bcu gnyis po de dag ni // nyon mongs pa dang / las dang / bsdug bsngal rnams su 'du bar shes par bya'o // ni zhes bya ba'i sgras ni lhag pa'i tshig gcad pa'i tha tsig ste // mdo sde las bstan pa'i chos 'di dag las / gzhan cung zad kyang myed do zhes gcad[13] pa'o //

drisd pa de dag ni shes na // nyon mongs dpa' dang / las dang sdug bsngal 'di dag las gang 'byung ba ston cig //

smras pa / *gsum las gnyis 'byung ste* // nyon mongs pa zhes bya ba gsum po de dag las las shes bya ba gnyis 'byung ngo // *gnyis las bdun 'byung* ba ni // sdug bsngal zhes gong du bstan pa rnams so' // *bdun las* yang *gsum 'byung* ba ni // nyon mongs pa[14] zhes bya ba rnams so'[15] // nyon mongs pa gsum po dag las kyang gnyis 'byung ste / *srid pa'i 'khor lo*

1 Stein 621.2 and 622 "yin ba", not "yin pa".

2 Stein 621.2 "bsdug bsngal du" but preceded by something which has been erased. Stein 622 "sdug du". Here "sdug bsngal du" would be expected.

3 Stein 621.2 "bya". Stein 622 "bya'".

4 Stein 622 "rnam par". Stein 621.2 "rnams par".

5 Stein 622 "skye mched". Stein 621.2 "skye mced".

6 Stein 622 "rnams so". Stein 621.2 "rnams so'".

7 In Stein 622 this double shad is in fact: a shad, followed by a design of three circles, and a shad. In Stein 621.2 this double shad is in fact: a shad, followed by a design of four circles, and a shad, all in both black and red. Above, these markers in Stein 622 were not reflected in Stein 621.2. Also this marker does not mark a quotation.

8 Stein 622 "bsdu ba ste". Stein 621.2 "bsdus ste".

9 Stein 621.2 "sdug pa". Stein 622 "sdug".

10 Stein 621.2 "rnams su". Stein 622 "rnams".

11 In Stein 622 this double shad is in fact: a shad, followed by two vertical circles, and a shad.

12 Significantly Stein 622 does not continue in a neat and tidy fashion but jumps what appears to be a substantial gap. Nevertheless even the Tibetan numbering treats the text as continuous, the next folio we have is the second, "gnyis", though the first folio did not have the word "gcig". Our source for the following is Stein 621.2. Stein 621.2 omits the expected "bcu gnyis chos ni gsum du 'dus //".

13 In Stein 621.2 something has been erased from the middle of "gcad".

14 In Stein 621.2 "nyon na mongs pa" is written.

15 In Stein 621.2 the " 'a chung" here is below "so".

*de nyid ni 'khor*d ro // sred pa[1] ni gsum ste // 'dod pa dang / gzugs dang / gzugs myed pa' zhes bya'o // myi gnas pa thog ma nas 'jug pa'i 'khor lor gyurd pa // so so'i skye bo'i

[2]pa gsum 'byung ste // shing rta'i 'khor lo bzhin[3] du 'gyur[4] ba'o // bdag myed ces bya ba ni mu stegs can gyi bdag myi[5] yod pas // chos thams cad bya shes pa ni brdzun gyi // phyi nang gyi chos thams cad rgyu dang 'bras bu'i tshul bzhin gnas po'o // myi 'pho zhes pa ni 'ci ba'i char gtogs pa las brten te // skye ba'i char gtogs par[6] 'byung mod kyi // 'chi ba'i char gtogs pa de las / skye ba'i char gtogs par rdul tsam yang ma 'pho so / lus las bzlog pa mi rten cing[7] 'brel par 'byung ba'i snying po mjug na / yang zhes bya ba las 'cad de // dngos po rnams la myi rtag dpa' dang stong pa dang sdug bsngal bar rtogs na // dngos po la gti myi mug ces bshad pa la stsogs pa' / 'bri ti dang sbyar ro / 'di yan lag du mgo nan du bshad pa lags //

« snying po zhes bya ba ni // »[8]

'dus byas dang / 'dus ma byas kyi chos thams cad [9] 'dir 'dus pas na snying po'o // snying po 'di las mdo sde 'di yan lag mang por spror rdung bas na yang snying po'o //

« rten cing 'brel par 'byung ba zhes bya ba ni // »

[10]rgyu rnam pa gnyis 'brel pa[11] las / phyi nang gi[12] chos thams

1 Stein 621.2 "sred pa" but "srid pa" would be expected.

2 Stein 621.2 continues with 3a [76a]; but this next part is not an obvious or smooth continuation. The Tibetan numbering of the whole of Stein 621 suggests a gap, our 76 is 13 ("pa") while our 75 which precedes it is 8 ("nya").

3 In Stein 621.2 the "bzha" of "bzhin" is squeezed in below the line.

4 In Stein 621.2 " 'gyudr" is written.

5 In Stein 621.2 this "myi" is virtually erased.

6 In Stein 621.2 something more is written below the line, perhaps "pa'r" is the combined result.

7 In Stein 621.2 "mi rten cing" and not the expected "myi rten cing" with its "ya btags". This is the only occurrence of "mi" in any of our Stein texts and is clearly not "myi" in Stein 621.2.

8 Text found between these chevrons or guillemets français appears in red ink in Stein 621.2. Red ink was not used in the appropriate places earlier.

9 In Stein 621.2 something has been erased here.

10 Stein 622 recommences here, with its second folio, [54a], and with Tibetan numbers in words for the rest of the text.

11 In Stein 621.2 "sa /" has been crossed out.

12 Stein 622 "gi". Stein 621.2 "gyi".

cad 'byung ste / rgyu rnam pa gnyis po de yang gang zhe na / gtso bo'i rgyu dang byed pa grogs su gyur pa'i[1] rgyu'o // de la nang gi[2] gtso bo'i rgyu[3] ni rnam par shes pa dang[4] bcas pa'i las dang / nyon mongs pa'o // byed pa grogs su gyur pa'i[5] rgyu ni pha ma la stsogs pa'o // yang gzhan du na gtso bo'i rgyu ni[6] /[7] ma rig pa nas rga shi'i bar du'o // byed pa grogs su gyur pa'i[8] rgyu ni chen po bzhi'o // rgyu 'di rnams ma tshang ba[9] myed pa las / mying [10]dang gzugs kyi[11] myi gu la stsogs pa[12] ma lus par 'byung ba[13] la bya'o // phyi'i rgyu gnyis po gang zhe na / sa bon ni gtso bo'i rgyu'o // khams drug ni [14]byed pa grogs su gyur pa'i[15] rgyu ste // rgyu 'di rnams ma tshang ba[16] myed pa las myu gu[17] la stsogs pa 'byung bar 'gyur ro //

« yan lag ces »[18] bya ba ni // mtshan nyid dang / byed pa'i stsal tha dad pa'i phyir na yan lag ces bya ste // dper na shing rta'i 'khor lo dang 'dra'o // gzhan du yan lag ces bya ba ni / 'phel ba[19] dang / 'phangs pa

1 Stein 622 "gyur pa'i". Stein 621.2 " 'gyur ba'i".
2 Stein 622 "nang gi". Stein 621.2 "gang gi".
3 Stein 621.2 adds "dang". Stein 622 omits it.
4 In Stein 622 this "dang" appears below the line.
5 Stein 622 "gyur pa'i". Stein 621.2 " 'gyur ba'i".
6 In Stein 622 a small cross marks the addition of "gtso bo'i rgyu ni" by means of an interlinear insertion.
7 In Stein 621.2 something other than a shad was attempted here.
8 Stein 622 "gyur pa'i". Stein 621.2 " 'gyur ba'i".
9 Stein 622 has the "ba" of "tshang ba" below the line. Stein 621.2 has "tsang ba" and something has been crossed out in the middle of "tsang", perhaps the beginning of a "ma".
10 In Stein 621.2 a letter has been crossed out here, perhaps the beginning of a "ga".
11 Stein 621.2 "kyi". Stein 622 "gyi".
12 Stein 621.2 "la stsogs pa". Stein 622 "las stsogs pa".
13 Stein 622 " 'byung ba". Stein 621.2 "byung ba".
14 In Stein 621.2 [upper left corner of 77a] there once appeared something like "Ch.73.VII.9 [48]" in red ink, but it has been erased and crossed out in black ink.
15 Stein 622 "gyur pa'i". Stein 621.2 " 'gyur ba'i".
16 Stein 622 "tshang ba". Stein 621.2 "tsang ba".
17 Stein 622 "myu gu". Stein 621.2 "myi gu".
18 Text found between these chevrons or guillemets français appears in red ink in Stein 622. It is interesting that red ink was not used in the appropriate places earlier in Stein 621.2 or 622, before the apparent gap, above. Here Stein 621.2 gives the whole phrase in red ink: "« yan lag ces bya ba ni // »".
19 Stein 622 " 'phel ba". Stein 621.2 " 'phen pa".

dang / mngon bar[1] sgrub pa[2] dang / bsgrubs pa[3] dang / nyes pa'i yan lag go // de la 'phel ba[4] ni ma rig pa dang / 'du byed dang / rnam par shes pa'o[5] // 'phangs pa ni mying dang gzugs dang / skye mched[6] drug dang / reg pa dang tshor ba'o[7] // mngon bar sgrub pa[8] ni sred pa dang len pa dang srid pa'o // bsgrubs pa ni skye ba'o // nyes pa ni [9]rga shi'o //

« bcu gnyis shes pa[10] / » [11]ni bcu gsum du yang[12] myi dgos / bcu gcig gis kyang myi chog[13] pas / gnyis dang[14] bcu ni bcu gnyis so //

« thub pa zhes bya ba / » ni lus dang / ngag thub pa la bya'o // yid thub pa ma smos pa ni dbang po'i rigs zhan pa'i rnams bkri ba'i[15] don la gzhag pa'i[16] phyir ma smos so // snod du gyur pa zhig na yid khongs nas phyung ste / yid thub pa zhes kyang bya'o //

« gsungs shes bya ba / » ni gsungs pa[17] bshad pa bstan pa las stsogs pa'i[18] tshig gi rnam grangs can du bsabs so[19] //

1 Stein 621.2 and 622 have "mngon bar", not "mngon par".
2 Stein 622 "sgrub pa". Stein 621.2 "bsgrub pa".
3 Stein 622 "bsgrubs pa". Stein 621.2 "bsgrub pa".
4 Stein 622 " 'phel ba". Stein 621.2 " 'phen pa".
5 Stein 622 "rnam par shes pa'o". Stein 621.2 "rnam par shes pa rnams so".
6 Stein 622 "skye mched". Stein 621.2 "skye mced".
7 In Stein 621.2 it would appear that part of an " 'a chung" was begun, then the "ba" was remembered and then that was followed by the " 'a chung" and the "na ro" in their proper sequence.
8 Stein 622 "sgrub pa". Stein 621.2 "sgrub pa pa".
9 In Stein 621.2 something has been erased here, which looks like a "sha".
10 Stein 622 "shes pa". Stein 621.2 "shes pa'".
11 In Stein 621.2 "ba" has been crossed out.
12 Stein 622 "yang". Stein 621.2 omits it.
13 Stein 622 "chog". Stein 621.2 "cog".
14 Stein 622 "dang". Stein 621.2 "dang dang", though the second "dang" has been slightly erased.
15 Stein 621.2 "bkri ba'i". Stein 622 "bkra'i ba'i".
16 In Stein 621.2 this is written "gzhzhag pa'i" but the first "zha" has been crossed out in red, though it is quite difficult to see that this has happened.
17 Stein 622 "gsungs pa". Stein 621.2 "gsungs pa'".
18 Stein 622 "las stsogs pa'i". Stein 621.2 "las / stsa / stsogs pa'i", an error not crossed out.
19 Stein 621.2 has an abbreviated "bsabso" for "bsabs so". Stein 622 "bas so".

« dris pa rkyen[1] gyi bye brag[2] de[3] dag ni so sor shes na / gang du bsdu ba blta ba thos par 'dod do // »

smras pa / rkyen gyi bye[4] brag bcu gnyis po de dag ni gsum du 'dus te[5] / « nyon mongs pa dang las dang sdug [6]bsngal ba'o // » de la sdug bsngal thams cad kyi[7] rtsa ba bas na nyon mongs pa'o // 'du byed gsum po mngon bar byed cing / 'jig rten gzhan du skye bar gdon myi za bar[8] srid pa bas na las so // myi bde ba thams cad tshor bas myang bar 'gyur bas na sdug bsngal lo // « gsum du ji [9]lta ba bzhin zhes bya ba ni / » nyon mongs pa dang / las dang / sdug bsngal bar ma lus pa'i don to //

« dris pa[10] / bcu gnyis gsum du bsdus pa ni shes na / nyon mongs pa'i nang du ni du dang gang / las gyi nang du ni du dang [11]gang /[12] sdug bsngal ba'i nang du ni du[13] dang gang[14] / gang du 'gro ba ston cig // »[15]

smras pa / nyon mongs pa'i nang du gsum ste / ma rig pa dang / sred pa dang / len pa'o[16] // las gyi nang du ni gnyis ste // 'du byed dang srid pa'o // sdug bsngal gyi nang du ni bdun te[17] / rnam par shes pa[18] / mying dang

1 Stein 622 "rkyen". Stein 621.2 "rgyen".

2 In Stein 622 the " 'greng bu" of "bye brag" is so much a part of the "gi gu" of "gyi" that it at first glance seems as if the spelling here is "bya brag".

3 In Stein 622 "de" may well have been written over an erased "ni"; certainly the traces of a "gi gu" can be seen.

4 In Stein 622 the " 'greng bu" of "bye brag" is more or less non-existent, the "gi gu" of "gyi" serving as a short form for one syllable with "gi gu" and one syllable with " 'greng bu".

5 Stein 622 " 'dus te". Stein 621.2 " 'dus ste".

6 In Stein 621.2 a letter has been erased here; it looks like a "sa".

7 Stein 621.2 "kyi". Stein 622 "gyi".

8 Stein 622 "za bar". Stein 621.2 "za' bar".

9 In Stein 621.2 a further letter precedes "lta" here, probably the beginning of a "ba".

10 Stein 622 "« dris pa »". Stein 621.2 "« dris pa' »".

11 In Stein 622 [upper left corner of 55a] there once appeared something like "Ch.51.I.23 [40]" written in red but it has been erased.

12 Stein 622 "« las gyi nang du ni du dang gang / »". Stein 621.2 omits this.

13 In Stein 622 the "da" of "du" is written, or rewritten, in black ink.

14 In Stein 622 the "nga" of "gang" is placed below the "ga" not beside it, and is written in black ink.

15 In Stein 622 this double shad is in fact: a shad, followed by a design of four circles, and a shad, all in red ink.

16 Stein 622 "len pa'o". Stein 621.2 "len pa / da'o" as well as something which has been erased, perhaps five syllables or so.

17 Stein 622 "bdun te". Stein 621.2 "bdun ste".

18 Stein 622 "shes pa". Stein 621.2 "shes pa'".

gzugs / skye mched[1] drug / reg pa / tshor ba / skye ba[2] rga shi rnams so // « ni zhes bya ba ni / » bsdu ba'i tha tsig ste / sdug bsngal brgyad dang / gsum dang gzhan dag kyang ngo[3] // « chos bcu gnyis po de dag ni gsum du 'dus // » gong du smos pa'i nyon mongs pa dang / las dang / sdug bsngal bar 'dus pa la bya'o // « ni zhes bya ba ni / » lhag pa'i tshig[4] gcad pa'i tha tshig[5] ste // mdo sde'i don dag las gzhan na myed par bstan pa dang / grangs bcu gnyis su chad pa'o // 'di yan cad[6] rgyu rkyen la rag lus pa'o //[7]

« dris pa gang gi nang du gang bsdu ba ni shes na / nyon [8]mongs pa dang / las dang sdug bsngal 'di dag gang las gang 'byung ba ston[9] cig // »

smras pa nyon mongs pa gsum las / las shes bya ba gnyis 'byung ste // [10]ma rig pa la 'du byed 'byung // sred pa [11] dang len pa gnyis las / srid pa 'byung // las gnyis las sdug bsngal bdun 'byung ste // 'du byed las rnam par shes pa[12] nas tshor ba'i bar du lnga 'byung // srid pa las skye ba dang rga shi gnyis 'byung[13] / sdug bsngal bdun las / yang nyon mongs pa gsum 'byung ste // rnam par shes pa nas tshor ba'i[14] bar du lnga las / sred pa dang len pa gnyis 'byung / mying dang gzugs nas tshor ba'i bar du bzhi ste / skye[15] ba dang / rga shir mying brjes ste / ma 'ongs pa'i skye ba dang / rga shi de las[16] sred pa dang len pa 'byung // sred pa[17] dang

1 Stein 622 "skye mched". Stein 621.2 "skye mced".
2 Stein 622 "skye ba". Stein 621.2 omits it. In Stein 621.2 "sha" has been crossed out.
3 Stein 621.2 "kyang ngo". Stein 622 "kyango", an abbreviation of "kyang ngo".
4 Stein 622 "tshig". Stein 621.2 "tsigs".
5 Stein 622 "tha tshig". Stein 621.2 "tha tsig".
6 In Stein 621.2 "cad" is written over top of an erased word.
7 In Stein 622 this double shad is in fact: a shad, followed by a circle, and a shad.
8 In Stein 621.2 something has been erased here.
9 Stein 622 "« ston »". Stein 621.2 "« stond »".
10 In Stein 621.2 a "ra" has been erased here.
11 In Stein 622 both "gi gu" and " 'greng bu" are found — "sreid pa" — signifying perhaps indecision between writing "sred pa" and "srid pa" which was never clarified.
12 Stein 622 "rnam par shes pa". Stein 621.2 "rnam par shes".
13 In Stein 622 this " 'byung" appears to be written below a crossed out word.
14 In Stein 621.2 the "tsha" is quite badly formed but the slightly askew strokes show clearly the order for forming a handwritten "tsha".
15 In Stein 622 this "skye" is written below the line.
16 In Stein 621.2 the "sa" of "las" is added below the line.
17 Stein 622 "sred pa". Stein 621.2 "srid pa".

len pa[1] 'das pa[2] ma rig par 'gyur[3] bas na / de ltar sdug bsngal bdun las / nyon mongs pa gsum 'byung ngo //

« yang zhes bya ba ni / » tshul bzhin yid[4] la ma byas pas / yang dang yang du 'khor ba la bya'o //

« 'khor ba zhes bya ba ni / » srid pa'i gnas so // srid pa ni gsum ste / 'dod pa dang / gzugs dang /gzugs myed pa'o //

« 'khor lo de nyid ces bya ba ni / » srid pa'i bdag nyid du 'gyur ba la bya'o // « 'phyan ces bya ba ni / » don myed pa la bya'o // « ni zhes bya ba ni / » nges pa myed par bstan pa ste / las legs nyes gyis gnas mthon dman[5] du 'chol par[6] skye ba la bya'o // 'di yan cad thog ma[7] dang tha ma myed par bstan pa'i le'u'o //

« dris pa de ltar gang la gang 'byung ba ni shes na /

'o na lus thams cad kyi[8] dbang po sems can zhes bya ba gang yin / de'i[9] byed pa ci lta bu[10] //[11]

'gro ba thams cad ni / rgyu dang 'bras bu ste // gzhan gang yang sems can zhes bya ba myed do // »[12] de la [13]rgyu dang 'bras bu shes pa[14] de[15] ni gang zhe na // gang snga ma snga ma ni rgyu / phyi ma phyi ma[16] ni 'bras bu'o // yang gcig du na / nyon mongs pa dang / las gnyis rgyur gyur[17] pa

1 In Stein 621.2 something has been erased from the middle of the "len" of "len pa", perhaps a "da".

2 Stein 622 " 'das pa". Stein 621.2 " 'das pa'" followed by the traces of a "ra" which has been erased.

3 Stein 622 " 'gyur". Stein 621.2 "gyurd".

4 Stein 622 "tshul bzhin yid". Stein 621.2 "tsul bzhin du yid".

5 Stein 622 "dman". Stein 621.2 "man".

6 In Stein 621.2 the "cha" is quite badly formed but the strokes show the order for forming a handwritten "cha".

7 Stein 622 "thog ma". Stein 621.2 "thog pa ma".

8 Stein 621.2 "« kyi »". Stein 622 "« gyi »".

9 Stein 622 "« de'i »". Stein 621.2 "« ba de »".

10 The writing in red ink ends here in Stein 622, though it continues in Stein 621.2.

11 In Stein 622 this double shad is in fact: a shad, followed by a design of circles, and a shad.

12 In Stein 621.2 the writing in red ink ends here, though it ended earlier in Stein 622.

13 In Stein 621.2 a "da" is written here. Stein 622 does not have it.

14 Stein 621.2 "shes pa". Stein 622 "zhes pa".

15 In Stein 622 this "de" is inserted below the line.

16 Stein 622 "phyi ma phyi ma". Stein 621.2 "gang phyi ma 'phyi ma".

17 Stein 622 "gyur". Stein 621.2 "gyurd".

las / sdug bsngal bdun 'bras bur bstan pa'i tshul du'o // yang gcig du na / ma rig pa ni rgyu / 'du byed ni 'bras bu ste / de bzhin du rga shi'i bar du'o // de lta bas na / btags pa tsam du ma gtogs so // btags pa tsam la gnas na ni rdzas myed par myi rdung ngo[1] //

rnam pa de[2] bzhi'i tshul gyis [3]na[4] / sems can zhes bya ba myed do //[5] 'di yan cad[6] bdag myed pa'i le'u'o //[7]

« dris pa sems can zhes bya ba myed na / 'o na 'jig rten[8] 'di nas las legs nyes kyis[9] gnas mthon dman du skye ba ni su // stong pa'i[10] kho na las stong pa'i chos rnams 'byung bas[11] // » 'jig rten gzhan du[12] rdul tsam yang myi 'pho'o[13] // nyon mongs pa dang / las gnyis stong par gyur pa[14] las // sdug bsngal bar[15] brjod pa chos stong pa bdun 'byung ngo // yang gcig du na / ma rig pa stong pa las / 'du byed stong pa 'byung ba nas[16] / rga shi'i bar du de bzhin no // yang gcig du na shes pa skye ba dang // dgra[17] bcom ba srid pas na ma rig pa stong par mngon no // « mdzes par klog pa[18] dang / mkhas pas shes par bya'o // zhes pa'i[19] bar du ni 'bri ti dang sbyar te bshad

1 Stein 622 "rdung ngo". Stein 621.2 perhaps "rdungo", an abbreviation for "rdung ngo"?
2 Stein 622 "de". Stein 621.2 omits it.
3 In Stein 621.2 a "ga" has been crossed out.
4 Stein 622 "na". Stein 621.2 "na'".
5 In Stein 622 this double shad is in fact: a shad, followed by two vertical circles, a shad, followed by two vertical circles, and a shad.
6 Stein 621.2 "yan cad". Stein 622 "yan".
7 In Stein 622 this double shad is in fact: a shad, followed by one circle, and a shad.
8 In Stein 622 "rten" is inserted below the line, in black ink.
9 Stein 621.2 "nyes kyis". Stein 622 "nyes gyis".
10 Stein 622 "« stong pa'i »". Stein 621.2 "« stong pa »".
11 Stein 621.2 "« *'byung bas* »". Stein 622 "« *'byung ba bas* »" but the "« *ba* »" has been crossed out in black ink.
12 Stein 622 "gzhan du". Stein 621.2 "du".
13 Stein 622 " 'pho'o". Stein 621.2 " 'pho'a'o", i.e. " 'pho" + " 'a chung" + " 'a chung" with "na ro".
14 Stein 622 "gyur pa". Stein 621.2 " 'gyur bas". In Stein 621.2 something has been erased between the " 'a chung" and the "ga" of " 'gyur".
15 In Stein 621.2 "bar" is added below the line.
16 Stein 622 " 'byung ba nas". Stein 621.2 " 'byung ba la na".
17 Stein 621.2 "dgra". Stein 622 "dgra'".
18 Stein 622 "klog pa". Stein 621.2 "glog pa".
19 Stein 621.2 "zhes pa'i". Stein 622 "zhe sa'i".

do // » 'di yan cad myi 'pho bar bstan pa'i le'u'o //[1] « yang zhes bya ba ni / » 'khor ba las bzlog[2] par bshad de[3] // 'bri ti dang sbyar ro //

rten cing 'brel par 'byung ba'i snying po bshad pa'i brjed byang // rdzogs so[4] //[5]

* * * * *

1 In Stein 622 this double shad is in fact: a black shad, followed by two vertical red circles, and a black shad.

2 In Stein 621.2 something has been erased from between the "ba" and the "za" of "bzlog", possibly a "la".

3 Stein 622 "de". Stein 621.2 "do".

4 Stein 621.2 "rdzogs so'". Stein 622 "rdzogs". In Stein 621.2 the " 'a chung" here is below "so".

5 Stein 621.2 and Stein 622 end here. In Stein 621.2 this double shad is in fact: a shad in black and red, a shad in black and red, followed by a design of four circles in red only, and a shad in black and red.

Comments

The Dunhuang texts available which shed light on Nāgārjuna's Pratītya-samutpādahṛdayakārikā consist of one manuscript of the Pratītyasamutpāda-hṛdaya-kārikā in the Pelliot collection, seven incomplete manuscripts of the Pratītyasamutpādahṛdayavyākhyāna in the Pelliot collection, four incomplete manuscripts of the Pratītyasamutpādahṛdayavyākhyāna in the Stein collection and two incomplete manuscripts of the Pratītyasamutpāda-hṛdayavyākhyānābhismaraṇa also in the Stein collection.

If it is accepted that Pelliot 765 and Stein 621.1 (the first part of Stein 621) are in fact one manuscript divided between Paris and London then we do have one complete manuscript of the Pratītyasamutpādahṛdaya-vyākhyāna.

The Tibetan manuscripts of our texts in the Stein collection are among the manuscripts obtained by Sir Marc Aurel Stein on his second expedition to Central Asia in 1906-1908.

During the first World War Louis de La Vallée Poussin was living in Cambridge and at that time compiled his catalogue of the literary manuscripts in the Stein collection with the help of Miss C. M. Ridding.[1] By the time this was published all except the final volume of F. W. Thomas' Tibetan literary texts and documents concerning Chinese Turkestan[2] had appeared, and superseded any catalogue of those documents. The original plan had been to have one single publication of Thomas' and La Vallée Poussin's descriptions.

More recently the Seminar on Tibet[3] at the Tōyō Bunko has produced a catalogue of the Stein manuscripts based upon the Tōyō Bunko's microfilm.[4] For each manuscript it provides, in its first eight volumes, the

1 La Vallée Poussin, Louis de; Catalogue of the Tibetan manuscripts from Tun-huang in the India Office Library, London, 1962.

2 London, 1935–1963.

3 Tōyō Bunko Chibetto Kenkyū Iinkai.

4 Yamaguchi, Zuihō; Sutain shūshū Chibettogo bunken kaidai mokuroku, [A catalogue of the Tibetan manuscripts collected by Sir Aurel Stein], Part 1– , Tokyo, 1977–

number from La Vallée Poussin's catalogue as a heading, and then —

1) The microfilm reel number, the location on the microfilm, the Arabic folio numbers added to the manuscripts in London and the individual frame numbers of the film.
2) The original number.[1]
3) The Tibetan title.[2]
4) The number in the reprint of the Peking edition of the Tibetan Tripiṭaka, its volume number and the page number, number of the folio on that page and line number for the beginning and for the end of the text. Sometimes this is followed by the Arabic folio numbers added to the manuscripts in London, given in greater detail where it is thought to be helpful.
5) The Chinese title.[3]
6) The Taishō number, its volume and page numbers.
7) The Sanskrit title.[4]
8) The beginning and the end of the text, reproduced in Tibetan script.
9) Space for details of:
   a) related Stein collection material
   b) related Pelliot collection material
   c) relevant published material
   d) other points.

1 The original number given by Stein either as the items were discovered, acquired or unpacked. This begins with a "site-mark" namely the initial letter of the site, which for each of our manuscripts is "Ch." for Ch'ien-fo-tung, the Caves of the Thousand Buddhas at Dunhuang. Lower case Roman numerals refer to bundle numbers of bundles searched at Dunhuang. All of our final running numbers begin "00" signifying that the number was added at the time of unpacking at the British Museum. (Running numbers beginning "0" were given at the site.)

2 In squarish brackets where it is not supplied in the manuscript, and also within round brackets where it is newly supplied by the editors of the catalogue.

3 In squarish brackets where it is not supplied in the manuscript.

4 Romanised and within squarish brackets where it is not supplied in the manuscript. In Tibetan script where it is found in the manuscript.

A table covering the material in the first eight volumes of the catalogue matches the numbers from La Vallée Poussin's catalogue to the microfilm reel number, the location on the microfilm, and the individual frame numbers of the film.[1]

A table covering the complete collection of Tibetan manuscripts gives a clear overview of the volume numbers, the folio numbers, the numbers from La Vallée Poussin's catalogue and the original Stein numbers.[2]

What has been published is not the final version of this catalogue; it is intended that a revised — and no doubt more complete and detailed — edition will later be published in the light of readers' comments and further work.

The Tibetan manuscripts of our texts in Paris in the Pelliot collection are among the manuscripts obtained by Paul Pelliot on his expedition to Central Asia in 1906–1908. Though he came to Dunhuang after Stein he was given much greater liberty to examine manuscripts as he pleased, rather than having them brought to him.

A catalogue of the Tibetan manuscripts in the Pelliot collection was compiled by Marcelle Lalou and began to be published in 1939.[3]

In Lalou's catalogue our texts are placed in the section covering individual texts[4] including *madhyamika*, with the exception of Pelliot 114A which is found among the collected texts.[5]

In La Vallée Poussin's catalogue our texts are placed in the śāstra section — texts translated from an Indian treatise.

Most of our texts are on cut sheets of Tang paper, in pothī format,[6] usually with one or two holes for string to be threaded to keep the pages in order. Circles are usually drawn marking round where the holes are to be

1 Op. cit., Part 1, p. vii-xviii.

2 Op. cit., Part 12, p. 144–183.

3 Lalou, Marcelle; Inventaire des manuscrits tibétains de Touen-houang conservés à la Bibliothèque Nationale, (Fonds Pelliot n°s 1–849), Paris, 1939.

4 "Les textes isolés".

5 "Recueils".

6 Tibetan "po ti". Pelliot 762 is the exception, written on the back of a Chinese scroll.

placed which helps to guide the writer. The writing is dbu can.[1] The number of lines varies from three to six and extensive interlinear text is sometimes found. Both black and red ink are used, red ink often serving to mark out quotations. Many of the leaves are numbered either in Tibetan numbering or in Tibetan letter numerals, recto and on the left.

The orthography of these manuscripts is quite striking. The two forms of 'a chung — ordinary and flagged,[2] reversed gi gu, the use of da drag, the use of ya btags, extra 'a chung, and other wide variants in spelling are all encountered.

Where no pattern or consistency has been detected variations are not noted. For example flagged 'a chung and reversed gi gu are not pointed out because the variant uses — either in any one text or between texts — do not appear to have any significance.[3] For readers keen to judge for themselves it would be wise to look either at the original manuscripts or microfilm copies. The varying legibility of the manuscripts makes this the safest course should anyone suddenly detect a pattern in either the use of flagged 'a chung or reversed gi gu.

Da drag, with the "da" displayed as a character, is found both within the commentarial text and in the quotations themselves just as would be expected.

Variations in ya btags are noted, but in this there is a pattern. To a large extent in individual manuscripts of these particular texts if "mye" for "me",[4] "myed" for "med", "myi" for "mi" or "mying" for "ming" are found, then "me", "med", "mi" and "ming" are not found elsewhere in the manuscript. Unfortunately even this is not an absolute rule, but it is the norm. It would appear that, allowing for the occasional exception, in our texts any "ma" followed by a " 'greng bu" or "gi gu" will require "ya btags".

1 Headed. Where there are interlinear glosses the writing can be much more casual but generally it is not dbu med (headless).

2 A little flag or small hook curling towards the right, attached to the top right hand corner of the character, as with ordinary "tsa", "tsha" and "dza".

3 Akira Fujieda's theory that reversed gi gu is written most often while what now seems ordinary gi gu is written when another mark occurs closely on the left does not seem to apply to our texts at all. (See his: The Tunhuang manuscripts, a general description, *Zinbun*, Kyoto : 1966: 9, p. 22.)

4 In "mar mye", "mye long" and "mye shel" as well as "mye" on its own.

Extra 'a chung is not used consistently. Ordinary 'a chung (in "mtha'", " 'chi ka'i sems" or the like) is consistent. Also 'a chung to represent a Sanskrit long vowel (e.g. "pra ti' tya sa mud pa' da hri da ya bya khya na" for Pratītyasamutpādahṛdayavyākhyāna) is found as consistently as in classical Tibetan, which means it is used regularly but not with great accuracy.

The use of "ba" after the nasal closing letters[1] "na" and "ma" where classical Tibetan would use "pa" as an affix to a verb stem is consistent in four words: "yin ba" for "yin pa", "ldan ba'i" for "ldan pa'i", "mngon bar" for "mngon par" and "dgra' bcom ba" for "dgra' bcom pa".[2]

Variants in spelling are widespread. It is difficult to judge where these are errors and where they are accepted variant spellings. At times any difference between aspirated and unaspirated "ka" and "kha", "ca" and "cha" or "tsa" and "tsha" seems to be ignored. Classical distinctions — such as when to use "gis" or "gyis" — often appear to be unheeded. In all of our texts "du" is found consistently, "tu" is not found at all.[3]

Sometimes in editing these texts the classical rule has been favoured against the manuscript, especially when it is unclear whether "kyi" or "gyi", "pa" or "ba", or the like were deliberately intended. Are we looking at manuscripts written at a time when these spelling variants would be considered trivial and of no significance, or are we looking at the errors of scribes still learning to write in Tibetan?

If imagination is allowed to run unchecked it might be imagined that in Stein 622 where the manuscript has "sreid pa" — both "gi gu" and " 'greng bu" attached to one syllable — the writer may have written "sred pa", been told by his teacher or proof-reader that there was an error of "sred pa" for "srid pa" in the manuscript (referring to the very odd use of "sred pa" in

1 Tibetan "rjes 'jug".

2 This seems to have a reliable pattern. In classical Tibetan "pa" and "ba" can seem to be interchangeable, though this is often not clear in western editions of Tibetan texts where the accepted practice is to read "ba" as "pa" or "pa" as "ba" according to which is correct, not according to which is written or printed. The same is true of "ka" and "ga", especially in forms with "ya btags" and "gi gu" ("kyi" / "gyi", "kyis" / "gyis"), just as the same can be true of "da" and "nga".

3 It could be argued that "tu" is encountered in our texts but is not clearly differentiated from "du" because the "zhabs kyu" forces the "ta" to have much the same form as a "da". Certainly no difference can be distinguished with assurance in these manuscripts.

"bcu pa ni sred pa ste" much earlier in the text), and then added a "gi gu" tentatively to the wrong "sred pa" and never sorted out the confusion. Similar errors look like the work of someone learning rather than the work of an experienced and accomplished scribe.

Often when a letter or syllable has been erased, marked or crossed out it can be seen to turn up in its appropriate place just to the right of the error. In Pelliot 114A " 'brel par 'brel par" is written for " 'brel par" in the main title of the text and each character of the first " 'brel par" is ticked with a red tick. Also a "lag" precedes a "yan lag" but both letters of the first "lag" are marked at the top as if to be crossed out. Also a "kha" precedes a "de kho na" with the "kha" (i.e. a "kho" before its "na ro" had been written) marked at the top as if to be crossed out. In Pelliot 766 "thu" precedes a "gsung" followed by a "thub" and the first "thu" has been crossed out. In Stein 620 a "par" is preceded by a crossed out "ra", suggesting the "ra" of "par" was begun in error before the "pa". In Pelliot 765 before a "ma yin" a "ya" has been begun suggesting the "ya" of "yin" was begun prematurely. In Stein 621.1 before a "zhes" a "sa" has been begun, suggesting the "sa" of "zhes" was begun in error before the "zha". In Stein 621.2 where a "pa las /" is expected a premature "sa" and the shad part of a "pas /" has been crossed out just before the "las /" appears.

In Pelliot 765 "la 'di la" is written where " 'di la" would be expected. In Pelliot 768 "nyid nying" is written where "nying" alone would be expected, though there is no obvious sign of the "nyid" being crossed out or marked as an error. Stein 620 has "rnams rnams" for "rnams". Stein 621.1 has "bya ba ba'i" for "bya ba'i", "brtaggs" for "brtags" and "las las" for "las". Also in Stein 621.1 there is a "sdug bsngal" where it looks as if "bsngal" was begun, ran into the circle marking the place for the hole in the folio, was erased and rewritten to the right of the circle.

In Stein 621.2 there is a "bcom ldan 'das" where it would appear that "bco" was written followed by the commencement of the "la" of "ldan", then the final "ma" of "bcom" was remembered, and finally "ldan" was written in its proper place. In Stein 621.2 "nyon na mongs pa" is found in error for "nyon mongs pa". In Stein 621.2 a "ba'o" is found where it would appear part of an " 'a chung" was begun, then the "ba" was remembered and then that was followed by the " 'a chung" and the "na ro" in their proper sequence. In Stein 622 "nyon nyo mangs pa" is found in error for "nyon mongs pa", the second "nya" begun in error and then its "na ro" may have led to the lack of a "na ro" in "mangs".

In Pelliot 769 there is a large red blot marking the beginning of a serious error which may have been to mark the folio for rejection.

There are many more similar clues pointing to the hypothesis that these manuscripts are the work of inexperienced writers, either fairly new to writing or, much more likely, professional scribes, possibly accomplished in writing in Chinese, but new to writing in the Tibetan script.[1]

Where we have two manuscripts of the same part of one of the texts variations of punctuation are not usually noted. As is the usual practice the edited text is placed artificially in paragraphs. Double shad is treated as end of sentence or phrase punctuation even where it serves to frame the end of one phrase with one shad and the beginning of another with the other shad. The occasional shad at the end of a line in the manuscript but without any grammatical significance, is not noted.

1 Cf. gNam babs ki dar ma (Fragment 42, lines 206–224) an altogether different Dunhuang document which appears to be "a rather inexpert writing exercise", one which was "abandoned unrevised when it had been spoiled by so many errors" according to Hugh Richardson's "The Dharma that came down from heaven": a Tun-huang fragment, p. 219 and p. 229.

The Verses on the Heart of Dependent Origination (Pratītyasamutpāda-hṛdayakārikā) are substantially the same as the versions found in the canon.

Pelliot 769 has no sign of numbering on its one folio. It measures 10.5 x 42.8 cm. There are six lines of writing on one side of the folio, the other side has no writing. Only black ink is used for writing.

With regard to string holes Pelliot 769 has one in the middle of the folio encircled in red. The folio has rough grey lined margins at each end and has six grey lines to guide writing on one side and five grey lines on the other blank side of the folio.

Pelliot 769 has flagged 'a chungs.

Reversed gi gu is found in Pelliot 769.

Pelliot 769 shows ya btags.

Often an extra 'a chung is found at the end of a syllable, frequently just before a shad in Dunhuang texts. This is especially common with "pa'" (Pelliot 769 "byas pa'", "brtags pa'", "brel pa'r") or "na'" (Pelliot 769 " mthong na'"). Such examples fit the idea that we have here traces of early Tibetan adding an 'a chung to syllables ending in vowels. In classical Tibetan this survives only where there might be ambiguity. For example "mtha'" where — if there was no second closing letter 'a chung — the prefixed letter[1] "ma" could be taken theoretically as the main letter with an understood "a", followed by a closing letter "tha" — "math" — though in practice "tha" is never a closing letter. The use of the 'a chung makes it quite clear that the prefixed letter is "ma" and the main letter is "tha" — "mtha'".

In Pelliot 769 there are variants in spelling. The manuscript has "slobs dpon" for the expected "slob dpon". This "sa" is not an unexpected second closing letter but it is different from classical Tibetan.[2] We also find

1 Tibetan "sngon 'jug".

2 Richardson in his "The Dharma that came down from heaven": a Tun-huang fragment, p. 229, finds "slobs pon" as an error in the gNam babs ki dar ma. It is a matter of opinion just how widespread a spelling needs to be before it is treated as an alternative rather than an error. In our texts "slobs pon", "slobs dpon" and "slob dpon" are all found.

Nāgārjuna's name in Tibetan spelt "klus bsgrub" rather than the expected "klu sgrub".

The tshegs in Pelliot 769 are consistently placed unusually low, at the height of the middle of the letters.

Cristina Scherrer-Schaub has provided a romanised transcription of the five lines of text on this one folio in her article: Un manuscrit tibétain des Pratītyasamutpādahṛdayakārikā de Nāgārjuna.[1] The article is well worth seeking out as it discusses the text in its context within Buddhist teachings, relates it to other texts of Nāgārjuna and considers whether the text should have seven or five verses. It also provides a photographic reproduction of Pelliot 769. The transcription notes reversed gi-gu (as opposed to ordinary gi-gu) but not flagged 'a chung (as opposed to ordinary 'a chung). To note variants in the form of a letter is a very fiddly process, but here it is done with almost no mistakes, and of course readers who read Tibetan will not need to trust the transcription alone.[2]

1 Scherrer-Schaub, Cristina Anna; Un manuscrit tibétain des Pratītyasamutpādahṛdayakārikā de Nāgārjuna, *Cahiers d' Extrême-Asia*, Kyōto : 1987; 3: 103–112. On p. 106 n. 18 she writes, "Il va sans dire cette trancription n'est pas une édition critique du texte." Her work takes into account the two Peking versions of the Tibetan text, Kajiyama's Zōbon "Innen shinron shaku" and standardised forms found in the Mahāvyutpatti.

2 Read "j*i*" for "ji" on her p. 108, line 4. "Le *gigu* inversé est transcrit par la lettre i en italique." (p. 106).

An Interpretation of the Heart of Dependent Origination (Pratītyasamutpādahṛdayavyākhyāna) is substantially the same as the versions found in the canon.

The original Tibetan numbering of the folios is not always as straightforward as it might be.

Pelliot 114A has no sign of numbering on the one folio relevant to the Pratītyasamutpādahṛdayavyākhyāna. It begins at the beginning of the text. The manuscript measures 9 x 44.8 cm. There are three lines of writing on each side of the folio. Presumably this spacious layout was in preparation for extensive interlinear text as found in Stein 623. Black and red ink are used.

Pelliot 762 is a single roll containing five pages or panels. There are no page numbers. The first page has its left hand side torn away. The text is written on the back of a Chinese roll containing two Daoist texts (Pelliot chinois 3327). The Tibetan text of this manuscript begins almost where the complete Tibetan text would begin. The manuscript measures 25.5 x 195 cm. There are five lines of writing on the first page, six lines of writing on the second and third, seven lines of writing on the fourth, and two lines of writing on the uncompleted fifth page. The first page is accompanied by extensive interlinear text, at times eleven or more lines deep, meandering all over the page. It often marks quoted text not with red ink but with combinations of shads and circles. Some black and some brownish-red ink were used to mark and connect the interlinear text, but only black ink is used for written Tibetan characters in this manuscript, never red ink.

Pelliot 763 is a single folio numbered 2 ["rten gnyis"],[1] though it begins at the beginning of the text. The manuscript measures 8.5 x 43.5 cm. There are five lines of writing on the first side of the folio and six lines of writing on the other side, accompanied by extensive interlinear text, at times four lines deep. Black and red ink are used.

Pelliot 764 is a single folio significantly torn away on the left and therefore it has no page number. When it was a complete folio it would have begun at the beginning of the text. What remains of the manuscript

1 Here "rten" stands for the title of the text: "rten cing 'brel par 'byung ba'i snying po rnam par bshad pa".

measures 7 x ca34 cm. There are four lines of writing on each side of the folio. Black and red ink are used.

Pelliot 765 is a single folio numbered 2 ["kha"], though it begins at the beginning of the text. It ends precisely where Stein 621.1 begins. The manuscript measures about 8 x 48 cm. There are four lines of writing on each side of the folio. Black and red ink are used.

Pelliot 766 consists of two folios, or three fragments as the second folio is clearly made up of two fragments, the left hand one in much poorer condition than the right hand one. It begins at the beginning of the text, or at least it would have done if the complete folios were there. Both folios are significantly torn away on the left. No Tibetan numbering is found on the folios. Arabic numbers "1" and "2" have been added to the left of the folios in Paris. The fragments give a measurement of 13 x ca38 cm. for the folios. There are three lines of writing on each side of the folios, accompanied by extensive interlinear text, at times ten or more lines deep. Black and red ink are used.

Pelliot 768 is a single folio numbered 4 ["nga"] beginning near the end of the text and ending at the end. The manuscript measures 7.6 x 51 cm. There are five lines of writing on one side of the folio accompanied by extensive interlinear text and one centred line at the top of the opposite side of the folio, a line containing the colophon. Only black ink is used for writing.

Stein 620 is a single folio numbered 1 ["ka"] but beginning mid-sentence perhaps three folios into the text and ending mid-sentence, perhaps originally having another two folios to the end of the text. The manuscript measures 7.5 x 50.8 cm. There are five lines of writing on each side of the folio. Black and red ink are used.

Stein 620 is clearly the Pratītyasamutpādahṛdayavyākhyāna and not the Pratītyasamutpādatriṃśakakārikāvyākhyāna which La Vallée Poussin took it to be.[1]

Stein 621.1 begins on folio 3a ["ga"], beginning precisely where Pelliot 765 ends. Stein 621.1 ends on folio 6a ["cha"]. The end on folio 6a is also the end of the text. The manuscript measures 8 x 48 cm. There are four lines of writing on each side of the folios, with the final side of the final folio left blank. Black and red ink are used.

1 La Vallée Poussin, Louis de; op. cit., p. 194.

Stein 623 is a single folio, unnumbered in Tibetan. It begins at the beginning of the text, but we have only these first two sides of the folio with such extensive interlinear text that the distance into the text is quite short. The manuscript measures 7.4 x 50.4 cm. There are three lines of writing on each side of the folio, with the interlinear text itself sometimes three lines deep. Black and red ink are used.

Stein 624 is a single folio numbered 4 ["bzhi"]. What remains of the manuscript measures 7 x 39 cm. There are five lines of writing on one side of the folio, two on the other. The text is often far from legible as there are extensive dark stains and the right edge of the folio has been torn off and apparently has not survived. Though it provides the text immediately before Pelliot 768 they cannot be two successive folios from a single copy of one specific manuscript as nothing else matches — the writing, the numbering, margins, precise folio size, string holes and so on. Black and red ink are used.

With regard to string holes in the various manuscripts, Pelliot 114A has one small string hole on the left half of the folio encircled in black. The folio has grey lined margins at each end and each side of the folio has five dark grey lines to guide writing.

Pelliot 762, being a roll, has no string holes but it does have black and brownish red lines to guide reading.

Pelliot 763 has one rough string hole with no circle around it. The folio has brownish red lined margins at each end and each side of the folio has six brownish red lines to guide writing.

Pelliot 764 has one string hole with a faint yellow or pale brown circle around it. Each side of the folio has yellow or pale brown margins (at the surviving right end) and five yellow or pale brown lines to guide writing.

Pelliot 765 has two string holes (not neat by any means, more of a tear than a hole on both folios) encircled in purplish red.

Pelliot 766 has one rough string hole encircled in red. Where it can be seen the folios have rough grey lined margins at each end and five or six grey lines to guide writing, on both sides of the folios. Some other vertical grey lines are also apparent.

Pelliot 768 has two string holes encircled in red. The folio has red lined margins at each end and has five grey lines to guide writing, on both sides of the folio.

Stein 620 has two neat large string holes encircled in red. The folio has red lined margins at each end.

Stein 621.1 has two string holes on each folio encircled in purplish red.

Stein 623 has two neat large string holes encircled in red. The folio has red lined margins at each end.

Stein 624 has one string hole in the middle of the folio, without any circle but space is left where the circle could have been written.

Pelliot 114A, 763, 764, 765, 766, 768, Stein 620, 621.1 and 624 have flagged 'a chungs. Pelliot 762 and Stein 623 have none at all.

Reversed gi gu is found in Pelliot 114A, 762, 763, 765, 766, 768, Stein 620, 621.1, 623 and 624. It is not found at all in Pelliot 764.

Da drag is shown in Pelliot 114A ("phyind pa'i", "gyurd pa", "bstand to"), Pelliot 762 " '*khor*d" and " 'khord ba'i".[1] Pelliot 763 ("gyurd pa"), Pelliot 765 (" 'gyurd pa'"), Pelliot 768 ("bstsald pa"), Stein 620 ("gyurd pa"), 621.1 (" 'gyurd", "gsold", "« '*khor*d »" and "bsald pa"), 623 ("gyurd pa") and 624 ("bstsald pa").

Da drag is also evident where it is not shown — rather than "slobs dpond kyis" Stein 623 has "slobs dpon kyis" and not "slobs dpon gyis". This is an example of da drag occurring much as it does in classical Tibetan even though no final "d" — in other words no second closing letter[2] "da" — is represented in the orthography. In classical Tibetan this can apply to the closing letters "na", "ra" and "la" followed by a second closing letter "da" which is no longer represented in the orthography, yet it still affects the initial letter of the next syllable. Here with "slobs dpon" closing letter "na" would suggest main letter[3] "ga" in "gyis", but instead an unseen second closing letter "da" causes main letter "ka" in "kyis" to follow. Da drag is of course a matter of orthography, the pronunciation remains the same whether or not the "da" is represented.

Pelliot 762, 763, 766, 768, Stein 620, 621.1 and 624 each show ya btags. Pelliot 114A, 764, 765 and Stein 623 do not, but nor do they have "me", "med", "mi", "ming", or any other word beginning with "ma" and followed by " 'greng bu" or "gi gu".

1 Interesting to note this is not " 'khord pa'i". (Italics are used to mark quotation in the commentary.)

2 Tibetan "yang 'jug".

3 Tibetan "ming gzhi".

Often an extra 'a chung is found at the end of a syllable, often just before a shad. This is especially common with "pa'" (Pelliot 114A, 762, 764, 766 and 768 "rnam par bshad pa'", Pelliot 766 "gyur pa'", Stein 620 "brjod pa'", 621.1 "ma rig pa'", "sred pa'", 624 "ngan pa'"), "na'" (Pelliot 766 "de kho na'", Stein 621.1 " 'tshal na'", 624 "de ltar na'") and "so'" (Stein 621.1 "rga shi rnams so'", 624 "myi chags so'"). It also occurs in a number of other circumstances.

In the middle of a syllable an extra 'a chung occurs less often. Pelliot 114A and Stein 623 have "bcom ldan 'da's", which is far from random given the relationship of the present form " 'da'" to the past " 'das", but we might have expected the closing consonant "sa" to have caused the 'a chung to be dropped.

Pelliot 114A, 764, 765 and Stein 623 have "yin bas" for "yin pas" and "ldan ba'i" for "ldan pa'i". Pelliot 762 has "yin ba" for "yin pa" and "ldan ba'i" for "ldan pa'i". Pelliot 763 has "yin bas" for "yin pas", "yin ba" for "yin pa", "ldan ba'i" for "ldan pa'i" and "phyin ba'i" for "phyin pa'i". Pelliot 766 has "[yin] bas" for "yin pas", "yin ba" for "yin pa" and "ldan ba'i" for "ldan pa'i". Pelliot 768 has "nor pa'i" for "nor ba'i" and "mngon bar" for "mngon par". Stein 620 has "yin ba" for "yin pa". Stein 621.1 has "yin ba" for "yin pa" and "mngon bar" for "mngon par". Stein 624 has none of these words in any form.

There are many variants in spelling. Pelliot 762, 764, 765, 768, Stein 623 and 624 have "la stsogs pa" as an alternative spelling of "la sogs pa". Pelliot 766 has "las stsogs pa". Pelliot 763 has "la bstsogs pa".

Pelliot 768 and Stein 624 have "bstsald pa" for "bsald pa" (as in Stein 621.1) or, if without da drag, for "bsal ba".

Pelliot 766 and Stein 621.1 have "skye mced" for "skye mched".

There are varying forms of "tshig" both on its own and in combinations. Pelliot 114A and Stein 623 have the expected "zur phyin pa'i tshig". Pelliot 762 has "[zur phyin] pa'i tshig", "tha tshig" and "tshigs". Pelliot 763 and 764 have the expected "zur phyin pa'i tshig" and "tha tshig". Pelliot 765 has "zur phyin pa'i tshigs" and "tha tshig". Pelliot 766 has "zur phyin pa'i tshig" and "tha tsig". Stein 620 has "tha tshig". Stein 621.1 has "tha tsigs", "tha tsig", "lhag ma'i tshig" and the like. Pelliot 768 and Stein 624 have "tshigs".[1]

1 Variations between "tshig" and "tshigs" where strictly speaking "tshig" is intended are common enough in classical Tibetan.

Stein 621.1 has " 'chi kha'i" as well as the expected " 'chi ka'i".[1]

Stein 620 has "shing tog skyur po'i skyus" and Stein 621.1 has "shing tog skyur po'i rgyus" but similar variants are also found in our canonical versions of the text.

Pelliot 762, 763, 766, 768, Stein 620 and 624 consistently have "srid pa" where it would be expected. Stein 621.1 has "sred pa" where "srid pa" would be expected, yet it also has "srid pa".[2]

Pelliot 766 has interesting aspirated sentence finals such as "... bstan tho" for "... bstan to" and "... yin the" for "... yin te".

Pelliot 114A has the expected "slob dpon". Pelliot 762 has "slobs dpon" and "slobs pon". Pelliot 763, 764, 765, 766, 768, Stein 621.1, 623 and 624 have "slobs dpon". Similarly Stein 621.1 has "stong pa", "stong" and "stongs pa" while Pelliot 762, 768, Stein 620 and 624 have "stong pa".

What look like abbreviations, from the point of view of classical Tibetan, are also found. Pelliot 114A, 762, 763, 764, 765 and 766 have "gzho nur" for "gzhon nur", while Stein 623 has "gzhonur" for "gzhon nur". Pelliot 765 has "gnyiso" for "gnyis so" and " 'byung bo" for " 'byung ba'o". Pelliot 762 has "rnamso" for "rnams so". Pelliot 762 and 766 have "rnamsu" for "rnams su" and "lasu" for "las su". Stein 621.1 has "maṃcis pa'i" for "ma mcis pa'i" a variant spelling of "ma mchis pa'i" and also has "rdzogs'o " for "rdzogs so". Pelliot 768 has "de 'is" for "de yis" and even "de dgi" for "de dag gi".

Pelliot 763 would be the best contender for a prime example of an inexperienced writer with weak spelling and poor concentration. Many of its oddities could hardly be argued as acceptable alternative spellings at any stage of the development of the Tibetan language. As already mentioned it has the most bizarre variant on "la sogs pa" with its "la bstsogs pa". Its unconventional use of aspirated and non-aspirated letters is quite impressive. It has "gthogs pa'o" for "gtogs pa'o", "gchig la gchig" for "gcig la gcig" and "mdung kyim" for "mdung khyim". It also has an intriguing "bcu gnyigs gyi" for "bcu gnyis kyi". A "bar" for "bsdu bar" suggests a syllable has been skipped. Many more examples could be cited.

Pelliot 762 is less extreme but includes "cud par" for "chud par", "rag

1 Another spelling variant common enough in classical Tibetan.

2 Confusion between "srid pa" and "sred pa" is common enough in classical Tibetan.

lus pa" an alternative for "rag las pa",[1] "mdod rgyal" for " 'dod rgyal", " 'jaṃ dpal" for " 'jam dpal", "gsuṃ po" for "gsum po"[2], "zhes par" for "shes par", "gchad pa'i" for "bcad pa'i", "thams chad gyi" for "thams cad kyi", "sems chan" for "sems can", "tsham" for "tsam", and "mci' " for "mchi", and so on.

In considering whether Pelliot 765 and Stein 621.1 are one manuscript divided between Paris and London a number of factors can be taken into account.

Stein 621.1 provides the text immediately following that of Pelliot 765, suggesting they could be two successive folios from a single copy of one specific manuscript, particularly as the break comes mid-sentence. The numbering fits well with Pelliot 765 numbered 2 ["kha"] and Stein 621.1 numbered 3 ["ga"] to 6 ["cha"]. The numbering is also striking because it is written in a relatively sloppy style and is placed higher in the left margin than might be expected.

The writing itself looks to be by the same hand and also has certain consistent idiosyncrasies. Looking at the manuscript with a view to judging the style various similarities become apparent. Restricting the examination to strokes above the line will give enough evidence. The flag on "tsa" and "tsha" often seems to sprout from the middle of the top of the letter and not the expected right hand side. Na ro is often far to the left when attached to "pa" "ma" and "sa" and far to the right when attached to "la", as if its position is decided by a vertical stroke in the main character. Both manuscripts display flagged 'a chung, and many other similarities.

The folio size appears to be the same. There are four lines of writing on each side of the folios. The two string holes with their purple circles match. Black shads are found shadowed by red shads in both manuscripts.[3]

Various other points could be made, but there seems no room for doubt that Pelliot 765 in Paris and Stein 621.1 (the first part of Stein 621) in London make up one complete manuscript copy of the Pratītyasamutpāda-hṛdayavyākhyāna text.

1 A variant found in later Tibetan also.

2 The anusvāra in these words is in the form of a relatively large circle.

3 An argument based on consistency of spelling could be put forward here but that would be weak in the general context of Dunhuang Tibetan language manuscripts where consistency of spelling is sometimes not found even within one sentence.

Clarification of an Interpretation of the Heart of Dependent Origination (Pratītyasamutpādahṛdayavyākhyānābhismaraṇa) is not found in the Tibetan Buddhist canon.[1]

The most striking thing about this text is that its citations of the original Pratītyasamutpādahṛdayakārikā verses are paraphrased; they are not literal quotations either in their grammar or in their vocabulary. The first part of the Pratītyasamutpādahṛdayavyākhyānābhismaraṇa follows the same layout and general content that the Pratītyasamutpādahṛdayavyākhyāna has, but again the grammar and vocabulary are not literal copies. However, after the gap in each of our manuscripts it takes on a character quite different to the Pratītyasamutpādahṛdayavyākhyāna.

The original Tibetan numbering of these folios is also not always as straightforward as it might be. Stein 621.2 begins on folio 7a ["ja"] and ends on folio 17a ["tsa"], but there are no folios 9, 10, 11 and 12. Folio 8b ends mid-sentence and folio 13a begins mid-sentence in the middle of a word, confirming the extensive gap. There are four lines of writing on each side of the folios, with three lines on the final side of the final folio, where the text seems to end quite naturally. Equally the beginning on folio 7a seems a quite natural beginning to the text. The manuscript measures 8 x 48 cm, the same size as Stein 621.1. Though Stein 621.1 and 621.2 are most definitely two texts it is easy to see why La Vallée Poussin treated them as one (621) in first assigning text numbers on the basis of the page numbering in Tibetan: 3–6, 7–8 and 13–17, the surviving folios of a straight run from 1 to 17. In pencil on the right side above the Arabic folio numbers which were added to the manuscripts in London ([70]–[80]) are the numbers 1–11.

Stein 622 begins with an unnumbered folio, followed by folios 2 ["gnyis"], 3 ["gsum"] and 4 ["bzhi"]. The manuscript measures 7.7 x 43.3 cm. There are five lines of writing on each side of the folios, with two lines on the final side of the final folio, where the text seems to end quite naturally. However, it is not as "complete" as La Vallée Poussin thought it to be.[2]

1 Or perhaps more correctly "has not yet been found".

2 La Vallée Poussin, Louis de; op. cit., p. 194.

It might appear that Stein 622 could be in fact two manuscripts, not one. The first folio has no number. The next three folios do have numbers. The second folio is not a continuation of the first but instead suggests a large gap. If the gap found in Stein 621.2 is of four folios then the gap in Stein 622 may well be of five folios.

But why should it not be accepted that the page numbering is in a sense incorrect, and Stein 622 is simply a first folio followed by perhaps folios 7, 8 and 9 of one manuscript? Page numbering need not necessarily have been written by the writer of the manuscript or when the manuscript was written. But as well as the inconsistency in the page numbering, most of the quotations on the first folio are marked by elaborate shads, which is not the case in the other three folios. Also the later three folios make use of red ink in writing quotations, but no red ink appears in the first folio.[1] It seems that while we have the beginning and end of one single text — the Pratītya-samutpādahṛdayavyākhyānābhismaraṇa — in Stein 622 we still might not have one single manuscript copy of the text, but rather two distinct manuscripts.[2] But on examining the writing for consistency and looking unsuccessfully for significant spelling variations, the balance clearly favours one manuscript, or at least one scribe. The variations in elaborateness of shads and use of red ink can be put down to the close parallel of the first part of the Pratītyasamutpādahṛdayavyākhyānābhismaraṇa with the Pratītya-samutpādahṛdayavyākhyāna, whereas the second part of the Pratītya-samutpādahṛdayavyākhyānābhismaraṇa ranges well away from the format of the Pratītyasamutpādahṛdayavyākhyāna.

With regard to string holes in the manuscripts, Stein 621.2 has two string holes on each folio usually encircled in purplish red.

Stein 622 has no string holes or accompanying circles, nor any space left for them. The folios have lined margins at each end.

Stein 621.2 and 622 (*i* and *ii*) both have flagged 'a chungs.

Reversed gi gu is found in Stein 621.2, but Stein 622 (*i* and *ii*) has none at all.

Da drag is shown in Stein 621.2 (" 'gyurd", "drisd pa", " '*khor*d ro", "gyurd pa" and "stond cig"), but Stein 622 (*i* and *ii*) has no examples of it.

1 Though blurring the issue a little, it should be noted that Stein 621.2 also has no red ink before its four folio gap.

2 Where it seems possibly significant we refer to folio 1 as Stein 622*i* and the final three folios, folios 2–4, as Stein 622*ii*.

Stein 621.2 and 622 (*i* and *ii*) show ya btags, though Stein 621.2 does have "mi rten cing" where "myi rten cing" would be expected.

In Stein 621.2 often an extra 'a chung is found at the end of a syllable, usually just before a shad. This is especially common with "pa'" (Stein 621.2 "ma rig pa'"), "ma" (Stein 621.2 "lhag ma'"), "na'" (Stein 621.2 "tshul gyis na'"), "so'" (Stein 621.2 "tha tsigs so'", rga shi rnams so') and "to'" (Stein 621.2 "bstan to'"). Also relevant is Stein 621.2 " 'dri 'a'o" with its two 'a chungs side by side ('dri then 'a chung + 'a chung with o). Stein 622 (*i* and *ii*) has no extra 'a chungs.

Stein 621.2 and 622 have "yin ba" for "yin pa", "mngon bar" for "mngon par", "ldan ba'i" for "ldan pa'i" and "dgra' bcom ba" for "dgra' bcom pa".

There are many variants in spelling. Stein 621.2 has "la stsogs pa" or "la stsogs pa'" and "las stsogs pa" as spellings of "la sogs pa". Stein 622 (*i* and *ii*) also has "la stsogs pa" and "las stsogs pa" as spellings of "la sogs pa", sometimes (Stein 622*i*) both occurring in the same sentence. Occurrences of either alternative vary in each text, and they do not necessarily match.

Stein 621.2 has "skye mced" for "skye mched" consistently. Stein 622 (*i* and *ii*) has "skye mched".

Stein 621.2 and 622 (*i*) have "skye bu" where "skyes bu" might be expected.

Stein 621.2 has varying forms of "tshig": "tha tsig", "tshig", "lhag pa'i tshig", "lhag pa'i tsigs", "zur phyin pa'i tsig" and the like. Stein 622 has "tha tsig" (*i* and *ii*), "tha tshig" (*ii*), "tshig" (*ii*), "lhag pa'i tshig" (*ii*), "zur phyin pa'i tshig" (*ii*) and the like.

Stein 621.2 as well as "sdug bsngal" has "bsdug bsngal", presumably a "ba" written as a premature commencement of "bsngal" and then never crossed out.

Stein 621.2 and 622 (*i*) have "sred pa" where "srid pa" would be expected, yet Stein 621.2 also has "srid pa". Stein 621.2 also has "srid pa" where "sred pa" would be expected. Stein 622 (*ii*) consistently has "srid pa" where it would be expected, though the unusual "sreid pa" for "sred pa" mentioned above occurs in Stein 622 (*ii*).[1]

1 See p. 122 and 131 above.

Stein 621.2 has "slobs dpon" for the classical "slob dpon". Stein 622 (*i*) has "slob dpon" and "slobs dpon".

Stein 621.2 has considerable variations in punctuation from Stein 622 (*i* and *ii*), but these are not noted shad by shad.

Background to the Dunhuang Texts

Though we might place Nāgārjuna in the second century, our Tibetan canonical versions of his texts in translation are printed from blocks carved in the eighteenth century.[1] Even the original compiling of the first printed Tibetan canon may take us back no further than the thirteenth century. Tibetan manuscript sources, where they exist, can take us further back in time.[2] From the seventh century onwards there are Tibetan translations of Buddhist texts which later will become Tibetan canonical texts. Dunhuang texts let us remove a large part of that chronological gap in the Tibetan sources which we can read and that strengthens their value for use alongside Sanskrit manuscripts where we have them.[3]

Dunhuang is in the province of Gansu in northwestern China. Significantly it is at what was once the intersection of great trade routes passing through Central Asia. The bulk of China lies to the east, Mongolia to the north, Tibet to the south and routes leading as far as India and the Near East lie to the west.

It is well known that Tibetan troops were involved in Xinjiang and points east at varying times from the middle of the seventh century for a period of about three hundred years and various districts came under

1 Peking bstan 'gyur c1724. sNar thang bstan 'gyur c1732. sDe dge bstan 'gyur c1733. The Co-ne bstan 'gyur is thought to have been carved a few years after the sDe dge.

2 Indeed Pelliot mentions among the texts at Dunhuang a ninth century Tibetan bka' 'gyur of which he purchased three volumes. (See his: Une bibliothèque médiévale retrouvée au Kan-sou, *BEFEO*, Hanoi : 1908: 8.501–529).

3 With regard to the Sanskrit manuscripts of the Pratītyasamutpādahṛdayakārikā and part of the Pratītyasamutpādahṛdayavyākhyāna, the Kashmiri manuscript is taken by Gokhale to be in Gilgit script of the sixth or seventh century (Gokhale, Vasudev; Encore: the Pratītyasamutpādahṛdayakārikā of Nāgārjuna, p. 64) and the Lhasa manuscript is known to have been in existence in the fourteenth century in the collection of the Indian paṇḍit Lokottara (Gokhale, Vasudev; Der Sanskrit-Text von Nāgārjuna's Pratītyasamutpādahṛdayakārikā, p. 102).

The Ngor Sanskrit manuscript of the Mahāyānaviṃśikā is taken by Tucci to be in śaradā characters of the eighth or ninth century (Tucci, Giuseppe; Mahāyāna-viṃśikā of Nāgārjuna, p. 195).

Tibetan administration in the period when Tibet was one of the major powers in Asia. During the time of Tibetan administration Tibetan/Chinese bilingualism was common for both political and religious reasons. Dunhuang was part of this Tibetan empire from about 781 until 847. Before and especially after this period it was a relatively remote and inaccessible outpost of Chinese culture. Near the end of the period of Tibetan domination Buddhism in China suffered the destruction of monasteries and their contents in the Huichang persecution of 845. Dunhuang was unaffected by this persecution. And even when the Tibetans were finally ousted by Zhang Yichao Buddhism remained in favour there, with new cave temples being opened by Zhang Yichao himself.

Buddhism had flourished at Dunhuang for more than four centuries under the Chinese. The Master Mahāyāna[1] was invited to the Tibetan court from Dunhuang less than two hundred years after Srong btsan sgam po had been the first royal patron of Buddhism in Tibet. Srong btsan sgam po's sixth successor, Khri srong lde btsan, had invited Indian teachers such as Śantarakṣita and Padmasambhava to come to Tibet, and Buddhism was by this time more than just an interest of the royal court. The Master Mahāyāna came to represent one strand of Buddhist thinking, a position differing from the Buddhist teachings of Śantarakṣita and those of Padmasambhava. In other words someone from Dunhuang is seen to be at the centre of religious controversy as well as political affairs in Tibet, given the intertwining of the two which eventually led to the famous debate at bSam yas. The Master Mahāyāna and his followers may have lost that debate to Kamalaśīla (Śantarakṣita's pupil) and his followers — at least according to later Tibetan tradition — but whatever the case he returned to Dunhuang where he remained active in both religion and politics.[2]

During the Tibetan period at Dunhuang translation certainly flourished in the area. Indeed Chos grub (or Fa cheng in Chinese, perhaps

1 Chinese: He shang Mo he yan, Tibetan: Hva shang Ma hā yā na. Sanskrit: Upādhyāya Mahāyāna.

2 Demiéville, Paul; Le concile de Lhasa, une controverse sur le quiétisme entre Bouddhistes de l'Inde et de la Chine au VIIIe siècle de l'ère chrétienne, Paris, 1952. For a more recent treatment of the impact and significance of the great debate at bSam yas see David Seyfort Ruegg's Buddha-nature, mind and the problem of gradualism in a comparative perspective, London : School of Oriental and African Studies, 1989.

Dharmasiddhi in Sanskrit)[1] a translator at the Xiu dao si (Sūtra Temple) in Ganzhou[2] translated texts from Chinese into Tibetan and from Tibetan into Chinese. He translated the Sarvāstivādin Pañcavastukaśāstra into Chinese[3] in about 846 for example, two manuscripts of which survive as items found at Dunhuang.[4] From 833 until 838 he had lived and worked at Dunhuang.[5]

It is well established that there was a significant copying office at Dunhuang,[6] a fact which explains the huge numbers of multiple copies of Tibetan manuscripts such as the Aparimitāyus Sūtra[7] and Prajñāpāramitā texts. We also know the names of more than two hundred scribes of Tibetan texts working at Dunhuang. Other specific details are known such as the early ninth century donation which the Tibetan king Khri gtsug lde btsan (i.e. Ral pa can) made of 135 copies of the Aparimitāyus Sūtra in Chinese and 480 copies in Tibetan.[8] Details about payment for work done and even

1 Daishun Ueyama convincingly takes the view that Fa cheng was Chinese and lived in the Tibetan empire. See his: Daibankoku Daitoku Sanzō Hōshi Shamon Hōjō no kenkyū, [A study of the life and works of Fa-ch'eng (Ḥgo Chos grub) a translator of the Buddhist texts at Tunhuang under the Tibetan rule], *Tōhō gakuhō*, Kyōto : 1967; 38: 133–198, 1968; 39: 119–222. Paul Pelliot seems to take Chos grub to be a Tibetan rather than someone Chinese with a Tibetan name, in his Notes à propos d'un catalogue du Kanjur, *Journal asiatique*, Paris : 1914; 4: p. 142 f. Even if Pelliot had been correct it still would have illustrated the importance of the Tibetan language at the time. See also Tōru Haneda's Shakamuni Nyoraizō hōmetsujin no ki kaisetsu, *Shirin*, Kyōto : 1923; 8(1): 120–121; Juntarō Ishihama's Hōjō ni tsuite, *Shinagaku*, Kyōto : 1923; 3(5): 61–65 (379–383); and Tōru Haneda's Shogo, *Shinagaku*, Kyōto : 1923; 3(5): 65–68 (383–386).

2 Ganzhou had been captured by the Tibetans long before this time and even before Dunhuang, in about 766.

3 Sa bo duo zong wu shi lun.

4 Fonds Pelliot chinois 2073 and 2116. For the latter see chapter 9 of Paul Pelliot and Tōru Haneda's Manuscrits de Touen-houang conservés à la Bibliothèque Nationale de Paris et publiés par le Tōa-Kōkyūkwai de Changhai, Kyoto, 1926. Taishō 1556.

5 In the Yong gang si at Sha zhou (Dunhuang).

6 See Akira Fujieda's Bukkyōkai no ugoki, section 5 (p. 263–284) of his Toban shihaiki no Tonkō, *Tōhō gakuhō*, Kyōto : 1961; 31: 199–292.

7 I.e. the Amitāyus Sūtra.

8 Fonds Pelliot tibétain 999. This can be read easily in a good reproduction as Plate 308 in volume two of Ariane Spanien's superb Choix des documents tibétains conservés à la Bibliothèque Nationale, Paris, 1978–1979. See also Marcelle Lalou's Tun-huang documents on a Dharmadāna, *IHQ*, Calcutta : 1940; 16: 292–298 (then the manuscript was Fonds Pelliot tibétain n° provisoire 260).

details about the chasing up of bad debts are also available.[1]

Sanskrit texts among the hoard in the upright Gupta script of the Nepalese type[2] may well have arrived in Dunhuang by way of Tibet. This is the time when Tibet was engaged in a massive wholesale importation of Indian culture.

Paintings also reflect this period, both in Nepalese paintings of bodhisattvas which may well have come through Tibet and in Tibetan art itself. Some of the paintings on paper, such as one of a bodhisattva, perhaps Ākaśagarbha,[3] one of the arhat Kālika (painted by Do khon legs)[4] and one of the bodhisattva Vajrapāṇi,[5] include Tibetan inscriptions. A silk painting of Amitābha with the eight great bodhisattvas,[6] and a silk painting of the

1 Stein Tibetan MSS Tun Huang Collection Vol 56, folios 73–74 and Vol 69 folios 53–56 (Ch. 73. xv. 5). See F. W. Thomas' Tibetan literary texts and documents concerning Chinese Turkestan, part 2, p. 73–84 (Paper and copying of manuscripts).

2 Ch. 0079, for example, a Prajñāpāramitā text illustrated in Plate CXLII of Stein's Serindia, Oxford, 1921.

3 Ch. 00377. Colour Plate 48 in volume two of Roderick Whitfield's The art of Central Asia : the Stein collection in the British Museum, Tokyo, 1982–1985. The painting is also illustrated, but not in colour, on the left side of Plate XXXII in Stein's The Thousand Buddhas, London, 1921.

4 Ch. 00376. Colour Plate 49 in volume two of Whitfield's The art of Central Asia. The painting is also illustrated, but not in colour, on the right side of Plate XXXII in Stein's The Thousand Buddhas. The inscription shows an example of extra 'a chung as in our texts where it has "nyan thos chen po '" at the end of the first line on the right.

5 Ch. lvi. 002, one out of a set of ten. These banners would have been free to turn from a single suspension point and are therefore meant to be viewed from either side. In that sense the Tibetan inscriptions have been written on the reverse side, or at least the less well-finished side. For reading the inscriptions the best colour illustration of the reverse side is found as the frontispiece in Seiichi Taki's Tonkō Sembutsudō-shutsu Nipara-shiki sonzōga ni tsuite, *Kokka*, No. 399, p. 39–40, Tokyo, 1923. Colour Plates 48–1 and 48–2 in volume one of Whitfield's The art of Central Asia, are worth looking at as better colour illustrations than the chromoxylograph in Taki's article. The second plate gives the closest detail of the Tibetan script but to read the Tibetan the plates should be viewed with the aid of a mirror as they reproduce the front of the banner. The reverse of the painting is also illustrated in black and white in the upper left of Plate LXXXVII in Stein's Serindia.

6 Ch. 0074. Colour Plate 17 in volume one of Whitfield's The art of Central Asia.

Paradise of Bhaiṣajyaguru (painted by the monk dPal dbyangs in 836)[1] both include Tibetan inscriptions, and a maṇḍala of Avalokiteśvara according to the Amoghapāśadhāraṇī Sūtra has its invocation in Tibetan.[2] A silk painting of illustrations to the Vimalakīrti Sūtra shows a Tibetan king and his retinue in the audience below Vimalakīrti.[3] It is well worth comparing the colour plates of this with a photograph of the item before the bundle had been opened,[4] in order to gain some idea of the state of the materials when they were brought out of the walled up chapel. Either by the evidence of Tibetan inscriptions or on the strength of an undeniably Indian artistic style a significant part of the material can be assumed to date from the period of Tibetan rule.[5]

Our manuscripts are from amongst the collection taken from the walled up small room connected to the side of a cave shrine at the Caves of the Thousand Buddhas.[6] A hoard of paintings and texts were packed together

1 Ch. xxxvii. 004. Colour Plates 16–1 to 16–7 in volume one of Whitfield's The art of Central Asia, along with Figure 43, an infra-red photograph of the inscription in Chinese and Tibetan. The painting is also illustrated in black and white as Plate LIX in Stein's Serindia and in colour (only detail of the left side though it does include part of the inscription) as Plate III in Stein's The Thousand Buddhas.

2 Ch. xxii. 0015. Figures 50–51 in volume one of Whitfield's The art of Central Asia. Flagged 'a chuṇg and reversed gi gu are found in the invocation along with ordinary 'a chuṇg and ordinary gi gu. With regard to ya btags "myi" for "mi" is found.

3 Ch. 00350. Colour Plates 20–1 and especially 20–2 in volume one of Whitfield's The art of Central Asia.

4 Plate LXXVI in Stein's Serindia, top centre, "...silk painting (Ch. 00350) in original convolute state...".

5 The most unlikely Tibetan painting found at Dunhuang is one on hemp cloth, a painting of Tārā (sometimes taken to be a painting of Avalokiteśvara) which may well be a much later addition to the repository after it had been sealed up and then rediscovered, and which certainly seems to be a painting painted much later than the period of Tibetan domination at Dunhuang. It is the only painting in the hoard painted in tempera on a waxy ground over canvas.

Ch. lii. 001. Colour Plate 83 in volume two of Whitfield's The art of Central Asia and colour illustration Plate XXXI in Stein's The Thousand Buddhas. The painting is also illustrated in black and white in Raphaël Petrucci's Les peintures bouddhiques de Touen-Houang (mission Stein), *Annales du Musée Guimet, Bibliothèque de vulgarisation*, Paris : 1916; 41: 115–140, Plate VI (Figure 7); on p. 152 of Seiichi Taki's Toban-ga no shiryō ni tsuite, *Kokka*, Tōkyō : 1927; 439: 151–157; and in Joseph Hackin's A propos d'un article récent sur la peinture tibétaine, *Revue des arts asiatiques*, Paris : 1928; 5: 39–40, Figure 1 of Plate XVI (facing p. 40).

6 Qian Fo dong.

on a vast scale, neatly enough to suggest a repository of sacred material no longer in use rather than a hurried stash sparked by an invasion of the area, though the material had suffered careless treatment and the order of things was much disturbed. At the time the room was sealed the Tibetan manuscripts would have had little practical use yet they form the largest amount of material, at least by bulk, even greater than the Chinese.[1] Equally there were a number of things stored away which were in effect no more than sacred rubbish — carefully sewn up small bags of tiny scraps of inscribed paper, silk tapes, cloth wrappers and the like — and would not have been the most pressing choice for secure storage if the impetus was to save material from an invader. The considerable amount of secular material found reflects the sanctity accorded to the written word whatever the content, rather than weakening the case that this is a repository of sacred material.

It seems reasonable to assume our manuscripts found amongst this material were either written at or brought to Dunhuang somewhere between 781 and 847.[2]

Stein had heard from a trader about a rumour of this hidden deposit of manuscripts in one of the caves among the Caves of the Thousand Buddhas south-east of Dunhuang. The Daoist priest, Wang Yuanlu, had organised the restoration of one of the larger shrines and during the clearing of sand and débris from the cave temple a crack was noticed in a frescoed wall and investigation uncovered the room filled with packets of manuscripts in various languages including Sanskrit, Chinese, Khotanese, Sogdian, Uigur,

1 See p. 16 of Akira Fujieda's The Tunhuang manuscripts.

2 It is interesting to note that the index to āgama and śāstra literature in the lDan kar ma Palace in sTong thang suggests that the library contained the Pratītyasamutpāda-hṛdayakārikā and its Pratītyasamutpādahṛdayavyākhyāna at the time of Khri lde srong btsan (Sad na legs) (early ninth century). Specifically the Pho brang sTong thang lDan dkar gyi bka' dang bstan bcos 'gyur ro cog gi dkar chag by dPal brtsegs and others includes the items "rten cing 'brel par 'byung ba'i snying po'i tshig le'ur byas pa dang / de'i rnam par bshad pa / shlo ka lnga bcu rtsa gzhi /" (369a7–369a8) in its Mādhyamika śāstra section.

In Marcelle Lalou's edition of the text in her Les textes bouddhiques au temps du Roi Khri-sroṅ-lde-bcan, *Journal asiatique*, Paris : 1953; 241(3): 313–353, the entry is number 596. Lamotte has shown convincingly that the king is Khri lde srong btsan and not Lalou's Khri srong lde btsan (Lamotte, Étienne; La concentration de la marche héroïque (Śūraṃgamasamādhisūtra), Bruxelles, 1965, p. 109 ff.).

See also: Yoshimura, Shūki; The Denkar-ma: an oldest catalogue of the Tibetan Buddhist canons, Kyōto, 1950, where the entry is number 597.

and Tibetan.[1] The cave had been said to contain only manuscripts but on examination some bundles contained paintings on silk and on paper and even embroidered images. Bronze images and rubbings from stone inscriptions were also found there. The sealed room was good for preservation as it would have had a steady temperature, it was absolutely dry and the thinnest wall, the walled up entrance to the room, was covered by drifting sand for centuries. It would appear that the depositing of material in the room largely came to a halt in the early part of the eleventh century[2] and that the earliest of the dated material dates from the early fifth century.

On the expedition which brought our Stein manuscripts to Britain, about 500 paintings on silk, linen and paper, with prints and drawings on paper; about 150 pieces of textiles, embroidery, brocade, damask and gauze; and about 6,500 manuscripts and printed books were brought back from the Caves of the Thousand Buddhas.[3] The site at the Caves of the Thousand Buddhas was, of course, only one of many sites where materials were obtained by the expedition.

Paul Pelliot arrived in Dunhuang after Stein had left, and at first did not realize that Stein had examined material from the chamber and had taken away twenty-nine cases of its contents. Pelliot had heard of the manuscripts when he was in Urumchi where he had been shown an eighth century Chinese manuscript from Dunhuang which gave substance to the rumours he had heard about a large cache of manuscripts. Pelliot was an accomplished Sinologist and the Professor of Chinese at the École Française d'Extrême-Orient in Hanoi. He did not therefore suffer Stein's problem of choosing manuscripts without any knowledge of Chinese and could both judge what he was shown at Urumchi and could also converse with Wang Yuanlu in Chinese.

1 Figure 200 among the illustrations in Stein's Serindia shows the cave temple and the entrance to the room. Among the plans, Plate 43 (in vol III) shows the layout of the cave temple Ch.I. (Paul Pelliot's Grotte 163.)

2 When Stein first examined the contents of the room it had been open for at least eight years and Wang Yuanlu had added texts to the repository during that time as it was his most secure place for storage. Toshisada Naba suggests, in his Sembutsugan Bakkōkutsu– to Tonkō monjo (p. 25–27), that the manuscripts had been found there some sixteen or seventeen years before Stein's visit of 1907.

3 Guide to an exhibition of paintings, manuscripts, and other archaeological objects collected by Sir Aurel Stein, in Chinese Turkestan, London : British Museum, 1914, p. 3.

At Dunhuang Pelliot was allowed to work in the small room and examine everything.[1] He attempted to make at least a cursory examination of each item in the entire cache. He then persuaded Wang to sell him the items he judged most important and had them packed and sent to the Bibliothèque Nationale in Paris. He himself took a box of samples to Beijing and revealed the significance of the material to Chinese scholars and the authorities. This set in motion a process whereby the Beijing authorities attempted to place an embargo on the removal of the remaining contents of the cave.

* * * * *

Finally, returning to our main theme, it can be said that as a picture of the available work on the four texts — Nāgārjuna's Mahāyānaviṃśikā and his Pratītyasamutpādahṛdayakārikā with its Pratītyasamutpādahṛdaya-vyākhyāna and its Pratītyasamutpādahṛdayavyākhyānābhismaraṇa — has built up it is striking how much is available, yet further developments will add to our knowledge, hopefully making the texts more, not less, accessible to readers. It is worth mentioning that among all the sources for further enquiry into Nāgārjuna's work nothing comes close to Lindtner's Nagarjuniana as an overall guide to the literature, as well as its presentation of a number of texts. It would be the next place to turn to if the present work has sparked an interest.

1 Charles Nouette's photograph of Pelliot working by candlelight, crouching in the small room with the hoard of manuscripts towering above him is well worth seeking out. (Pl. CCCLXVIII "Touen-houang, — Grotte 163. Niche aux manuscrits" in Paul Pelliot's Les grottes de Touen-Houang, volume 6.) Pelliot's notes on the cave itself appeared in part 6 of Grottes de Touen-houang : carnet des notes de Paul Pelliot: inscriptions et peintures murales, volume 11 of Mission Paul Pelliot, documents conservés au Musée Guimet. (Grotte 163 : p. 19–20, p. 77-78 and pl. CCCLXVIII which is also found in this publication.)

Abbreviations

« »	Text found between these chevrons or guillemets français appears in red ink in the manuscript.
BEFEO	Bulletin de l'École Française d'Extrême-Orient
(C)	Co ne
Ch.	Ch'ien-fo-tung
(D)	sDe dge
IHQ	Indian Historical Quarterly
JIBS	Journal of Indian and Buddhist Studies
JRAS	Journal of the Royal Asiatic Society
(N)	sNar thang
N.S.	New Series
(P)	Peking
WZKS	Wiener Zeitschrift für die Kunde Südasiens und Archiv für Indische Philosophie

Bibliography

Throughout this work Tibetan texts are often listed with reference to the various editions available. Tibetan texts cited briefly in passing may only be provided with a reference to the Peking edition, chosen for this purpose as it is the most likely edition readers will have close to hand.

"Peking " refers to the reprint edition known as:

The Tibetan Tripiṭaka, Peking Edition [kept in the library of the Otani University, Kyoto] : reprinted under the supervision of the Otani University, Kyoto / edited by Daisetz T. Suzuki.
Tokyo-Kyoto : Tibetan Tripitaka Research Institute, 1955–1961.
168 vols. : ill.; 32 cm.
Japanese title: Chibetto Daizōkyō : eiin Pekin-ban.
Includes indexes.

The specific text numbers noted are those of this reprint.

"sNar thang" refers to a copy of the sNar thang edition of the bstan 'gyur kept in Cambridge University Library, (224 vols. : ill.; 13 x 66 cm.). The specific text numbers noted are those of Taishun Mibu's A Comparative List of the Tibetan Tripitaka of Narthang edition (bstan-ḥgyur division) with the sDe-dge edition, Tokyo, 1967.

"sDe dge" refers to the Delhi reprint of the sDe dge edition:

sDe-dge bsTan-'gyur Series published as part of the dGoṅs-rdzogs of H. H. The Sixteenth rGyal-dbaṅ Karma-pa.
Delhi : Delhi Karmapae Chodhey Gyalwae Sungrab Partun Khang, 1982–1986.
213 vols : ill. ; 11 x 65 cm.

The volume numbering of this series breaks with the long accepted numbering of Ui's catalogue for the sDe dge edition and the added pagination does not match the traditional Tibetan page numbering system. In order to avoid confusion my citations always use Tibetan volume numbers and Tibetan page numbers; it is therefore not necessary to have a particular version of the sDe dge edition in order to use a reference. Where appropriate the Tokyo reprint of the dbu ma section of the bstan 'gyur has also been used. It is part of the:

sDe dge Tibetan Tripiṭaka bstan 'gyur preserved at the Faculty of Letters, University of Tokyo.
Tōkyō : Sekai Seitan Kankō Kyōkai, 1977- .
31 x 22 cm.
Japanese title: Deruge-ban Chibetto Daizōkyō Ronshobu.
Includes indexes.

It follows quite normal practices, giving Tibetan volume and page numbers along with Ui's volume numbers and other helpful academic apparatus. The specific text numbers noted are those of Ui's Catalogue, i.e. the Tōhoku list numbers.

"Co ne " refers to the microfiche copy of the bstan 'gyur known as:

Tanjur. Cone edition.
The Tibetan Buddhist Canon, commentarial section : microfilmed from the volumes deposited at the Library of Congress.
Stony Brook : The Institute for Advanced Study of World Religions, 1974.
209 vols. on 2,226 microfiche : ill.
(IASWR Microform Series)

Taishō numbers refer to the:

Taishō Shinshū Daizōkyō / [revised, collated, added, rearranged and edited by J. Takakusu, K. Watanabe and G. Ono.
Tokyo : Society for the Publication of the Taisho edition of the Tripitaka], 1924–1934.
100 vols. : ill. ; 27 cm.
English title: The Tripiṭaka in Chinese.

Aiyaswami Sastri, N.
Ārya Śālistamba Sūtra, Pratītyasamutpādavibhaṅganirdeśasūtra and Pratītyasamutpādagāthā Sūtra / edited with Tibetan versions, notes and introduction, etc. by N. Aiyaswami Sastri.
Madras : Adyar Library, 1950.
[xlii], [111] p. ; 22 cm.
(Adyar Library Series ; 76)

Aiyaswami Sastri, N.
Nāgārjuna on the Buddhist theory of causation / [translated] by N. Aiyaswami Sastri.
p. 485–491 in the:
Professor K.V. Rangaswami Aiyangar commemoration volume.
Madras : [G.S. Press], 1940.
lxviii, 833 p. : ill. ; 26 cm.

Aiyaswami Sastri, N.
Nagarjuna's exposition of twelve causal links / [edited by] N. Aiyaswami Sastri.
Bulletin of Tibetology.
Gangtok : 1968; 5(2): 5–27.

Āryadeva II.
Caryāmelāyanapradīpa (i.e. sPyod pa bsdus pa'i sgron ma).
Peking bstan 'gyur — rgyud 'grel 33 (gi) (64a1–121b3) (2668).

Atīśa.
Bodhimārgapradīpapañjikā (i.e. Byang chub lam gyi sgron ma'i dka' 'grel) [His own commentary on his Bodhipathapradīpa].
Peking bstan 'gyur — mdo 'grel 31 (ki) (277b6–339b2) (5344).

Bapat, Pandurang Vaman.
Gilgit manuscripts and numerical symbols / by P. V. Bapat.
Journal of the Oriental Institute, Maharaja Sayajirao University of Baroda.
Baroda : 1961; 11(2): 127–131.

Bhattacharya, Vidhuśekhara.
Mahāyānaviṃśaka of Nāgārjuna : reconstructed Sanskrit text, Tibetan and Chinese versions with an English translation / edited by Vidhusekhara Bhattacharya.
Calcutta : Visvabharati Book-shop, 1931.

44 p. ; 25 cm.
(Visvabharati Studies ; 1)
(a reprint of his article in *The Visva-Bharati Quarterly*. Calcutta : 1930; 8: 107–150.)

Bhattacharyya, Benoytosh.
Two Vajrayāna Works [Prajñopāyaviniścayasiddhi by Anaṅgavajra and Jñānasiddhi by Indrabhūti] / edited with an introduction and index by Benoytosh Bhattacharyya.
Baroda : Oriental Institute, 1929.
xxi, 118 p. ; 24 cm.
(Gaekwad's Oriental Series ; 44)

Bhāvaviveka.
See: Bhavya.

Bhavya.
Madhyamakaratnapradīpa (i.e. dBu ma rin po che'i sgron ma).
Peking bstan 'gyur — mdo 'grel 17 (tsha) (326a6–365a3) (5254).

Bhavya.
Prajñāpradīpamūlamadhyamakavṛtti (i.e. dBu ma rtsa ba'i 'grel pa shes rab sgron ma).
Peking bstan 'gyur — mdo 'grel 17 (tsha) (53b3–326a6) (5253).

Candrakīrti.
Yuktiṣaṣṭikāvṛtti (i.e. Rigs pa drug cu pa'i 'grel pa).
Peking bstan 'gyur — mdo 'grel 24 (ya) (1a1–33b4) (5265).

Catalogue des manuscrits chinois de Touen-houang (Fonds Pelliot chinois).
Paris : Bibliothèque Nationale, 1970–
Vol. 1– : ill. ; 26 cm.
At head of title: Bibliothèque Nationale. Département des Manuscrits.

Demiéville, Paul.
Le concile de Lhasa, une controverse sur le quiétisme entre Bouddhistes de l'Inde et de la Chine au VIIIe siècle de l'ère chrétienne / par P. Demiéville.
Paris : Imprimerie Nationale de France, 1952.
398 p. : 32 plates ; 26 cm.
(Bibliothèque de l'Institut des Hautes Études Chinoises ; 7)

Dharmendra.
Tattvasārasaṃgraha (i.e. De kho na nyid kyi snying po bsdus pa).
Peking bstan 'gyur — rgyud 'grel 72 (nu) (87a6–110b8) (4534).

Dīpaṃkaraśrījñāna.
See: Atīśa.

dPal brtsegs; et al.
Pho brang sTod thang lDan dkar gyi bka' dang bstan bcos 'gyur ro cog gi dkar chag.
Peking bstan 'gyur — mdo 'grel 126 (cho) (352b5–373a8) (5851).

Dragonetti, Carmen.
On Śuddhamati's Pratītyasamutpādahṛdayakārikā and on Bodhicittavivaraṇa / by Carmen Dragonetti.
Wiener Zeitschrift für die Kunde Südasiens und Archiv für Indische Philosophie.
Wien : 1986; 30: 109–122.

Dragonetti, Carmen.
The Pratītyasamutpādahṛdayakārikā and the Pratītyasamutpādahṛdaya-vyākhyāna of Śuddhamati / by Carmen Dragonetti.
Wiener Zeitschrift für die Kunde Südasiens und Archiv für Indische Philosophie.
Wien : 1978; 22: 87–93.

Faber, Flemming.
A Tibetan Dunhuang treatise on simultaneous enlightenment: the *dMyigs su myed pa tshul gcig pa'i gzhung* / by Flemming Faber.
Acta Orientalia.
Copenhagen : 1985; 46: 47–77.

Ferrari, Alfonsa.
Arthaviniścaya / Alfonsa Ferrari.
Atti della Reale Accademia d'Italia. Memorie della Classe di scienze morali e storiche. Serie 7.
Roma : 1944; 4: [535]-625.

Fujieda, Akira.
Toban shihaiki no Tonkō [Tun-huang under the Tibetans] / Akira Fujieda.
Tōhō gakuhō.
Kyōto : 1961; 31: 199–292.

Fujieda, Akira.
The Tunhuang manuscripts, a general description / by Fujieda Akira.
Zinbun.
Kyoto : 1966; 9: 1–32, 1969; 10: 17–39.

Giles, Lionel.
Descriptive catalogue of the Chinese manuscripts from Tunhuang in the British Museum / by Lionel Giles.
London : Trustees of the British Museum, 1957.
xxv, 334 p. ; 28 cm.

gNubs-chen Saṅs-rgyas-ye-śes.
See under "n".

Gokhale, Vasudev.
Eine der im Sanskrittext verloren gegangenen buddhistischen Sūtren / aus dem Chinesischen übertragen von Vasudev Gokhale.
Chinesisch-deutscher Almanach für das Jahr 1930.
Frankfurt am Main : 1930; p. 61–75.
(Extracted from his: Pratītyasamutpādaśastra des Ullaṅgha kritisch behandelt und aus dem Chinesischen ins Deutsche übertragen. Bonn, 1930.)

Gokhale, Vasudev.
Encore: the Pratītyasamutpādahṛdayakārikā of Nāgārjuna / by V.V. Gokhale in collaboration with M. G. Dhadphale.
p. 62–68 (with plates) in:
Dhadphale, M. G.
Principal V.S. Apte commemoration volume / edited by M. G. Dhadphale.
Poona : Deccan Education Society, 1978
68 p. : 2 folded plates ; 22 cm.[1]

Gokhale, Vasudev.
Pratītyasamutpādaśastra des Ullaṅgha / kritisch behandelt und aus dem Chinesischen ins Deutsche übertragen von Vasudev Gokhale.
Bonn : Bonner Universitäts-Buchdruckerei, 1930.
[37] p. : 4 plates ; 28 cm.

S. G. Mahajan kindly provided me with a photocopy of this article which had eluded inter-library loans in this country. It includes photographic reproductions of the leaves of the Sanskrit manuscript.

Gokhale, Vasudev.
Der Sanskrit-Text von Nāgārjuna's Pratītyasamutpādahṛdayakārikā / V. V. Gokhale.
p. 101–106 in:
Spies, Otto.
Studia Indologica, Festschrift für Willibald Kirfel zur Vollendung seines 70. Lebensjahres / herausgegeben von Otto Spies.
Bonn : Orientalisches Seminar der Universität Bonn, 1955.
375 p. ; 22 cm.
(Bonner Orientalistische Studien, Neue Serie ; 3)[1]

sGra sbyor.
Peking bstan 'gyur — mdo 'grel 124 (ngo) (1a1–38a3) (5833).

Guide to an exhibition of paintings, manuscripts, and other archaeological objects collected by Sir Aurel Stein, in Chinese Turkestan.
London : British Museum, 1914.
58 p. : folded map ; 22 cm.

Hackin, Joseph.
A propos d'un article récent sur la peinture tibétaine / J. Hackin.
Revue des arts asiatiques.
Paris : 1928; 5: 39–40 and Plate XVI (facing p. 40).

Haneda, Tōru.
Shakamuni Nyoraizō hōmetsujin no ki kaisetsu / Tōru Haneda.
Shirin.
Kyōto : 1923; 8(1): 120–121, (with illustration on frontispiece to No. 1).

1 Vasudev Gokhale, through Mangala Chinchore, was very helpful in providing me with a photocopy of his transcript of the Lhasa manuscript used for this article.

If Giuseppe Tucci's notes on his Sanskrit manuscript of the Mahāyānaviṃśikā in Ngor could be traced they might well be interesting. It is possible that he had a complete copy of the manuscript made or that he might have photographed it. Apparently nothing can be traced by the Istituto Italiano per il Medio ed Estremo Oriente in Rome and on my own visit to Rome in 1986 nothing at all was unearthed.

More significantly if the two Sanskrit manuscripts could be examined in Tibet, assuming they have survived, they would provide much firmer ground for speculations about the original Sanskrit texts.

Haneda, Tōru.
Shogo / Tōru Haneda.
Shinagaku.
Kyōto : 1923; 3(5): 65–68 (383–386).

Haraprasād, *Śāstri.*
Bauddhagāna o dohā / Haraprasād Śāstri.
Kalikātā : Baṅgīya Sāhitya Parishat Mandira, 1323 [1916].
xxxvi, 210, cv p. : 11 plates ; 26 cm.
(Sāhitya pariṣad granthāvalī ; 55)
At head of title: Hājāra bacharera purāṇa Bāṅgālā bhāshāya.

Hatani, Ryōtai.
Daijō nijūju ron / Ryōtai Hatani.
p. 44–47 in:
Kokuyaku issaikyo, Chūganbu 3.
Tōkyō : Datō Shuppansha, 1932.
246 p. ; 23 cm.

Ishihama, Juntarō.
Hōjō ni tsuite / Juntarō Ishihama.
Shinagaku.
Kyōto : 1923; 3(5): 61–65 (379–383).

Jamspal, L.
The Pratītyasamutpāda-hṛdaya-kārikā-vyākhyāna of Nāgārjuna, reconstruction and translation into English from the Tibetan / L. Jamspal and Peter della Santina.
Buddhist studies. A yearly research journal of the Department of Buddhist Studies, University of Delhi.
Delhi : 1974; 1: [9]-24.

Kajiyama, Yūichi.
Chūganha no jūnishi engi kaishaku / Yūichi Kajiyama.
Bukkyō shisōshi.
Kyōto : 1980; 3: [89]-146.

Kajiyama, Yūichi.
Zōbon "Innen shinron shaku" / Yūichi Kajiyama.
p. 1–15 (i.e. 1–15 of the last sequence) in:
Bukkyō ni okeru seishi no mondai / Nihon Bukkyō Gakkai hen.
Kyōto : Heirakuji Shoten, 1981.
2, 517, 15 p. ; 22 cm.
(Nihon Bukkyō Gakkai Nenpō ; 46)

Lalou, Marcelle.
Inventaire des manuscrits tibétains de Touen-houang conservés à la Bibliothèque Nationale: Fonds Pelliot tibétain / M. Lalou.
Paris : Bibliothèque Nationale, 1939–1961.
3 vols. ; 28 cm.

Lalou, Marcelle.
Les textes bouddhiques au temps du Roi Khri-sroṅ-lde-bcan / par Marcelle Lalou.
Journal asiatique.
Paris : 1953; 241(3): 313–353.

Lalou, Marcelle.
Tun-huang documents on a Dharmadāna / M. Lalou.
Indian Historical Quarterly.
Calcutta : 1940; 16: 292–298.

Lamotte, Étienne.
La concentration de la marche héroïque (Śūraṃgamasamādhisūtra) / traduit et annoté par Étienne Lamotte.
Bruxelles : Institut Belge des Hautes Études Chinoises, 1965.
xiii, 308 p. ; 25 cm.
(Mélanges chinois et bouddhiques ; 13)

La Vallée Poussin, Louis de.
Bodhicaryāvatārapañjikā, Prajñākaramati's commentary to the Bodhicaryāvatāra of Çāntideva / edited with indices by Louis de La Vallée Poussin.
Calcutta : Asiatic Society, 1901–1914.
7 fascicules ; 23 cm.
(Bibliotheca Indica, New Series ; [150])

La Vallée Poussin, Louis de.
Bouddhisme, études et matériaux : théorie des douze causes / par L. de La Vallée Poussin.
Gand : Faculté de Philosophie et Lettres de l'Université de Gand, 1913.
ix, 128 p. ; 25 cm.
(Université de Gand, Recueil de travaux publiés par la Faculté de Philosophie et Lettres ; 40)

La Vallée Poussin, Louis de.
Catalogue of the Tibetan manuscripts from Tun-huang in the India Office Library / by Louis de La Vallée Poussin; with an appendix on the Chinese manuscripts by Kazuo Enoki.
London : Oxford University Press, 1962.
xviii, 299 p. : [4] p. of plates ; 29 cm.

La Vallée Poussin, Louis de.
Études et textes tantriques: Pañcakrama [attributed to Nāgārjuna. With the commentary of Parahitarakṣita] / par L. de La Vallée Poussin.
Gand : Faculté de Philosophie et Lettres de l'Université de Gand, 1896.
xv, 56 p. : 25 cm.
(Université de Gand, Recueil de travaux publiés par la Faculté de Philosophie et Lettres ; 16)

La Vallée Poussin, Louis de.
Madhyamakavṛttiḥ, Mūlamadhyamakakārikās (Mādhyamikasūtras) de Nāgārjuna avec la Prasannapadā commentaire de Candrakīrti / publiée par Louis de La Vallée Poussin.
St.-Pétersbourg : Imprimerie de l'Académie Impériale des Sciences, 1903–1913.
7 parts ; 25 cm.
(Bibliotheca Buddhica ; 4)

La Vallée Poussin, Louis de.
Notes et bibliographie bouddhiques / par L. de La Vallée Poussin.
Mélanges chinois et bouddhiques.
Bruxelles : 1932; 1: 377–424.

Lindtner, Christian.
Adversaria Buddhica / by Christian Lindtner.
Wiener Zeitschrift für die Kunde Südasiens und Archiv für Indische Philosophie.
Wien : 1982; 26: 167–172.

Lindtner, Christian.
Atiśas Introduction to Two Truths, and its sources / Chr. Lindtner.
Journal of Indian Philosophy.
Dordrecht : 1981; 9: 161–214.

Lindtner, Christian.
Nagarjuniana : studies in the writings and philosophy of Nāgārjuna / by Chr. Lindtner.
Copenhagen : Akademisk Forlåg, 1982.
327 p. : ill. ; 21 cm.
(Indiske Studier ; 4)

Macdonald, Ariane.
See: Spanien, Ariane.

Malan, Solomon Caesar.
Tibetan books and manuscripts of the late Alexander Csoma de Körös presented to the Royal Hungarian Academy of Sciences at Budapest / by S. C. Malan.
Journal of the Royal Asiatic Society. New series.
London : 1884; 16: 494.

Mibu, Taishun.
A comparative list of the Tibetan Tripitaka of Narthang edition (bstan-ḥgyur division) with the sDe-dge edition / compiled by Taishun Mibu.
Tokyo : [Taishō Daigaku], 1967.
[3], 142 leaves ; 24 x 35 cm.
Cover title: Taishō Daigaku shozō Chibetto Daizōkyō Narutan-ban Ronshobu mokuroku.

Mikogami, Eshō.
Innenshin ron ju ni tsuite [On the Pratītyasamutpādahṛdaya-Kārikā] / Eshō Mikogami.
Indogaku Bukkyōgaku kenkyū.
[*Journal of Indian and Buddhist Studies*]
Tōkyō : 1962; 10: 173–176 (577–580).

Naba, Toshisada.
Sembutsugan Bakkōkutsu to Tonkō monjo / Toshisada Naba. p. 11–68, [English summary: Chinese manuscripts from Tun-huang cave temples / by Toshisada Naba. p. 1–16] in:
Seiiki Bunka Kenkyūkai.
Tonkō Torufan shakai keizai shiryō; 1 / Seiiki Bunka Kenkyūkai hen.
Kyōto : Hōzōkan, 1959.
463, 27, 55 p. : ill. ; 31 cm.
(Seiiki bunka kenkyū ; 2)
[Chinese fragmentary manuscripts on social and economical system in the T'ang era unearthed from Tunhuang and Turfan; 1 / the Research Society of Central Asian Culture.
(Monumenta Serindica ; 2)]

Nāgārjuna.
Mahāyānaviṃśakā
— Tibetan bstan 'gyur editions.

Candrakumāra / Sha' kya 'od translation:

Peking - dbu ma 17 (tsa) (156a4–157a5) (5233)

sNar thang - mdo 17 (tsa) (146b3–147b3) (3224)

sDe dge - dbu ma 17 (tsa) (137b1–138a7) (3833)

Co ne - dbu ma 17 (tsa) (135a6–136a6)

Ānanda / Grags 'byor shes rab translation:

Peking - dbu ma 33 (gi) (211b8–213a1) (5465)

sNar thang - mdo 33 (gi) (202a8–203a6) (3456)

sDe dge - jo bo'i chos chung (178b6–179b3) (4551)

Nāgārjuna.
Pratītyasamutpādahṛdayakārikā
— Tibetan bstan 'gyur editions:

Peking - dbu ma 17 (tsa) (165b8–166a6) (5236)

sNar thang - mdo 17 (tsa) (156b2–156b7) (3227)

sDe dge - dbu ma 17 (tsa) (146b2–146b7) (3836)

Co ne - dbu ma 17 (tsa) (144a6–144b4)

and

Peking - dbu ma 33 (gi) (216a7–216b6) (5467)

sNar thang - mdo 33 (gi) (206a5–206b4) (3458)

sDe dge - jo bo'i chos chung (182a3–182a7) (4553)

Nāgārjuna.
Pratītyasamutpādahṛdayavyākhyāna
— Tibetan bstan 'gyur editions:

Jinamitra / Dānaśīla / Śīlendrabodhi / Ye shes sde, et al. translation:

Peking - dbu ma 17 (tsa) (166a7–168b3) (5237)

sNar thang - mdo 17 (tsa) (156b7–159a7) (3228)

sDe dge - dbu ma 17 (tsa) (146b7–149a2) (3837)

Co ne - dbu ma 17 (tsa) (144b4–146b4)

and

Peking - dbu ma 33 (gi) (216b6–219a6) (5468)

sNar thang - mdo 33 (gi) (206b4–209a2) (3459)

sDe dge - jo bo'i chos chung (182b1–184a5) (4554)

Nāgārjuna.
Yuktiṣaṣṭikākārikā (i.e. Rigs pa drug cu pa'i tshig le'ur byas pa).
Peking bstan 'gyur — mdo 'grel 17 (tsha) (22b2–25a7) (5225).

Nagy, Louis J.

Tibetan books and manuscripts of Alexander Csoma de Kőrös in the library of the Hungarian Academy of Sciences / by Louis J. Nagy.
p. 29–56 in:
Ligeti, Lajos.
Analecta Orientalia memoriae Alexandri Csoma de Kőrös dicata / edendo operi praefuit L. Ligeti.
Volumen 1.
Budapestini : Sumptibus Academiae Litterarum Hungaricae et Societatis a Csoma de Kőrös Nominatae, 1942.
224 p. ; 27 cm.
(Bibliotheca Orientalis Hungarica ; 5)

Naudou, Jean.
Les bouddhistes kaśmīriens au Moyen Age / Jean Naudou.
Paris : Presses universitaires de France, 1968.
242 p. : ill. ; 24 cm.
(Annales du Musée Guimet. Bibliothèque d'études ; 68)

gNubs-chen Saṇs-rgyas-ye-śes.
Rnal 'byor mig gi bsam gtan or Bsam gtan mig gron : a treatise on bhāvanā and dhyāna and the relationships between the various approaches to Buddhist contemplative practice / by Gnubs-chen Saṅs-rgyas-ye-śes; reproduced from a manuscript made presumably from an Eastern Tibetan print by 'Khor-gdoṅ Gter-sprul Chi-med-rog-'dzin.
Leh : Tashigangpa, 1974.
[169 p.] ; 28 x 38 cm.
(Smanrtsis shesrig spendzod ; 74)

Pelliot, Paul.
Une bibliothèque médiévale retrouvée au Kan-sou / par Paul Pelliot.
Bulletin de l'École Française d'Extrême-Orient.
Hanoi : 1908; 8: 501–529.

Pelliot, Paul.
Les grottes de Touen-Houang, peintures et sculptures bouddhiques / par Paul Pelliot.
Paris: Geuthner, 1920–1924.
6 vols. : plates, plans ; 33 cm.
(Mission Pelliot en Asie Centrale, Série in-quarto ; 1)

Pelliot, Paul.
Grottes de Touen-Houang : carnet de notes de Paul Pelliot : inscriptions et peintures murales / avant-propos de Nicole Vandier-

Nicolas / notes préliminaires de Monique Maillard.
Paris : Collège de France, Instituts d'Asie, Centre de recherche sur l'Asie centrale et la Haute Asie, 1981–1992.
6 vols ; 30 cm.
(Mission Paul Pelliot : documents conservés au Musée Guimet ; 11)
(Mission Paul Pelliot : documents archéologiques conservés au Musée Guimet ; 11)

Pelliot, Paul.
Manuscrits de Touen-houang conservés à la Bibliothèque Nationale de Paris et publiés par le Tōa-Kōkyūkwai de Changhai / sous la direction de P. Pelliot et T. Haneda.
Kyoto : [Tōa-Kōkyūkwai], 1926.
2 vols. ; 24 & 38 cm.
(Dunhuang yishu)
(Série in-folio I-IV, Série in-octavo I-IX)
Japanese title: Tonkō isho.

Pelliot, Paul
Notes à propos d'un catalogue du Kanjur / par Paul Pelliot.
Journal asiatique.
Paris : 1914; 4: 111–150.

Petrucci, Raphaël.
Les peintures bouddhiques de Touen-Houang (mission Stein) / par M. R. Petrucci.
Annales du Musée Guimet, Bibliothèque de vulgarisation.
(Conférences faites au musée Guimet en 1914).
Paris : 1916; 41: 115–140 (with plates).

Richardson, Hugh Edward.
"The Dharma that came down from heaven": a Tun-huang fragment / Hugh E. Richardson.
p. 219–229 in:
Kawamura, Leslie S.
Buddhist thought and Asian civilization, essays in honor of Herbert V. Guenther on his sixtieth birthday / edited by Leslie S. Kawamura and Keith Scott.
Emeryville : Dharma, 1977.
xviii, 307 p. : ill. ; 23 cm.

Ruegg, David Seyfort.
Buddha-nature, mind and the problem of gradualism in a comparative

perspective: on the transmission and reception of Buddhism in India and Tibet / by David Seyfort Ruegg.
London : School of Oriental and African Studies, 1989.
219 p. ; 22 cm.
(Jordan lectures in comparative religion ; 13)
At head of title: Jordan lectures 1987.

Schaeffer, Philipp.
Yukti-ṣaṣṭikā : die 60 Sätze des Negativismus / nach der chinesischen Version übersetzt von Phil. Schäffer.
Heidelberg : Harrassowitz, 1923.
21 p. : 6 p. of mounted facsimiles ; 25 cm.
(Materialien zur Kunde des Buddhismus ; 3)

Scherrer-Schaub, Cristina Anna.
Un manuscrit tibétain des Pratītyasamutpādahṛdayakārikā de Nāgārjuna / Cristina Anna Scherrer-Schaub.
Cahiers d'Extrême-Asia.
Kyōto : 1987; 3: 103–112.

Seminar on Tibet.
See: Yamaguchi, Zuihō

sGra sbyor.
See under "g".

Simonsson, Nils.
Indo-tibetische Studien : die Methoden der tibetischen Übersetzer, untersucht im Hinblick auf die Bedeutung ihrer Übersetzungen für die Sanskritphilologie / von Nils Simonsson.
Uppsala : Almqvist and Wiksells, 1957.
Vol. 1 (291 p.): ill. ; 25 cm.

Spanien, Ariane.
Choix de documents tibétains conservés à la Bibliothèque Nationale: complété par quelques manuscrits de l'India Office et du British Museum / présentés par Ariane Macdonald [Spanien] et Yoshiro Imaeda...
Paris : Bibliothèque Nationale, 1978–1979.
2 vols. : ill. ; 32 cm.
(Mission Paul Pelliot)

Staël-Holstein, *Baron* Alexander August von.
The Kāçyapaparivarta: a Mahāyānasūtra of the Ratnakūṭa class / edited in the original Sanskrit in Tibetan and in Chinese by Baron A. von Staël-Holstein.
[Shanghai] : Commercial Press, 1926.
xxvi, 234, [2] p. ; 27 cm.
Chinese title: Da bao ji jing Jia ye pin Fan Zang Han liu zhong he kan.

Stein, *Sir* Marc Aurel.
Serindia : detailed report of explorations in Central Asia and westernmost China carried out and described under the orders of H.M. Indian Government / by Aurel Stein.
Oxford : Clarendon Press, 1921.
5 vols. : ill., plates, maps, plans, facsimiles ; 35 cm.

Stein, *Sir* Marc Aurel.
The Thousand Buddhas : ancient Buddhist paintings from the cave-temples of Tun-huang on the western frontier of China / recovered and described by Aurel Stein / with an introductory es ay by Laurence Binyon.
London : Quaritch, 1921.
3 vols. : 48 plates ; 40 & 62 cm.

Takasaki, Jikido.
A study on the Ratnagotravibhāga (Uttaratantra) : being a treatise on the Tathāgatagarbha theory of Mahāyāna Buddhism including a critical introduction, a synopsis of the text, a translation from the original Sanskrit text in comparison with its Tibetan and Chinese versions, critical notes, appendixes and indexes / Jikido Takasaki.
Roma : Istituto Italiano per il Medio ed Estremo Oriente, 1966.
xiii, 439 p. ; 25 cm.
(Serie Orientale Roma ; 33)

Taki, Seiichi.
Toban-ga no shiryō ni tsuite / Setsuan Taki.
Kokka.
Tōkyō : 1927; 439: 151–157.

Taki, Seiichi.
Tonkō Sembutsudō-shutsu Nipara-shiki sonzōga ni tsuite / Setsuan Taki.
Kokka.
Tōkyō : 1923; 399: 37–40, (with plate).

Terjék, József.
Collection of Tibetan mss. and xylographs of Alexander Csoma de Körös / József Terjék.
Budapest : Magyar Tudományos Akadémia Könyvtára, 1976.
114 p. ; 24 cm.
(Keleti Tanulmányok ; 3)

Thomas, Frederick William.
Tibetan literary texts and documents concerning Chinese Turkestan / selected and translated by F. W. Thomas.
London : Royal Asiatic Society, 1935–1963.
4 parts ; 23 cm.
(Oriental Translation Fund, New Series ; 32, 37, 40, 41)

Tucci, Giuseppe.
Minor Buddhist texts / Giuseppe Tucci.
Roma : Istituto Italiano per il Medio ed Estremo Oriente, 1956.
xi, [311], xi, 289 p. ; 25 cm.
(Serie Orientale Roma ; 9)
Including:
Mahāyāna-viṃśikā of Nāgārjuna / [edited and translated by Giuseppe Tucci].
p. 195–207 (in section II of part I).
and :
Navaślokī of Kambalapāda / [edited and translated by Giuseppe Tucci].
p. 209–231 (in section III of part I).

Ueyama, Daishun.
Daibankoku Daitoku Sanzō Hōshi Shamon Hōjō no kenkyū / Daishun Ueyama.
[A study of the life and works of Fa-ch'eng (Ḥgo Chos grub) a translator of the Buddhist texts at Tunhuang under the Tibetan rule].
Tōhō gakuhō.
Kyōto : 1967; 38: 133–198, 1968; 39: 119–222.

Ui, Hakuju.
A complete catalogue of the Tibetan Buddhist Canons (bkaḥ-ḥgyur and bstan-ḥgyur) *and* A catalogue-index of the Tibetan Buddhist Canons (bkaḥ-ḥgyur and bstan-ḥgyur) / edited by Hakuju Ui, Munetada Suzuki, Yenshō Kanakura and Tōkan Tada.
Sêndai : Tōhoku Imperial University aided by the Saitō Gratitude Foundation, 1934.
2 vols. ; 29 cm.
Japanese title: Chibetto daizōkyō sōmokuroku.

Ui, Hakuju.
Engi shinju no zōkō hatten.
Chapter 2 (p. 235–271) of his:
Seiiki Butten no kenkyū / Hakuju Ui.
Tōkyō : Iwanami Shoten, 1969.
416 p. ; 22 cm.

Uryūzu, Ryūshin.
Innenshin ron (Engi no seiyō) / Ryūshin Uryūzu.
p. 355–365 in:
Yūichi, Kajiyama.
Daijō Butten 14, Ryūju ronshū / Kajiyama Yūichi, Ryūshin Uryūzu.
Tokyo : Chū Kōronsha, 1974.
426 p. ; 19 cm.

Uryūzu, Ryūshin.
Daijō nijūju ron (Daijō ni tsuite no nijū shiju) / Ryūshin Uryūzu.
p. 347–353 in:
Yūichi, Kajiyama.
Daijō Butten 14, Ryūju ronshū / Kajiyama Yūichi, Ryūshin Uryūzu.
Tōkyō : Chū Kōronsha, 1974.
426 p. ; 19 cm.

Vāsudeva Gokhale.
See: Gokhale, Vasudev.

Vidyābhūṣaṇa, Satis Chandra.
A descriptive list of works on the Mādhyamika philosophy, no. 1 / Satis Chandra Vidyābhūṣaṇa.
Journal and proceedings of the Asiatic Society of Bengal, New series.
Calcutta : 1910; 4: 367–379.

Vogel, Claus.
Vāgbhaṭa's Aṣṭāṅgahṛdayasaṃhitā, the first five chapters of its Tibetan [misprinted as "Tibṭean" in the first print run] version, accompanied by a literary introduction and a running commentary on the Tibetan translating-technique / edited and rendered into English along with the original Sanskrit by Claus Vogel.
Wiesbaden : Steiner, 1965.
viii, 298 p. ; 23 cm.
(Abhandlungen für die Kunde des Morgenlandes ; 37.2)

Whitfield, Roderick.
The art of Central Asia : the Stein Collection in the British Museum / Roderick Whitfield.
Tokyo : Kodansha in co-operation with the Trustees of the British Museum, c1982–1985.
3 vols. : chiefly ill. (some colour) ; 40 cm.

Yamaguchi, Susumu.
Nāgārjuna's Mahāyānaviṃśaka / [edited and translated by] Susumu Yamaguchi.
The Eastern Buddhist.
Kyoto : 1926; 4: 56–72, 1927; 4: 167–176.

Yamaguchi, Susumu.
Sthiramati : Madhyāntavibhāgaṭīkā : exposition systématique du Yogācāravijñaptivāda / édition d'après un manuscrit rapporté du Népal par Sylvain Lévi et précédée de sa préface par Susumu Yamaguchi.
Nagoya : Librairie Hajinkaru, 1934–1937.
3 vols. ; 25 cm.

Yamaguchi, Zuihō.
Sutain shūshū Chibettogo bunken kaidai mokuroku / [edited by] Yamaguchi Zuihō [and others, i.e. the Seminar on Tibet].
Tokyo : Toyo Bunko, 1977–
Part 1– ; 26 cm.
English title: A catalogue of the Tibetan manuscripts collected by Sir Aurel Stein.

Yoshimura, Shūki.
The Denkar-ma : an oldest catalogue of the Tibetan Buddhist canons / by Shuki Yoshimura.
Kyōto : Ryūkoku Daigaku Tōhō Seiten Kenkyūkai, 1950.
xviii, 72, 11 p.

Japanese title: Denkaruma mokuroku.
Available in a later reprint as p. 99–221 in:
Yoshimura, Shūki.
Indo Daijō Bukkyō shisō kenkyū / Yoshimura Shūki.
Kyōto : Hyakkaen, 1974.
605, 221 p. ; 22 cm.

Index